W9-AVY-066

Do-It-Yourselfer's Guide to
Furniture Repair & Refinishing
2nd Edition

TAB FURNITURE WOODSHOP SERIES

Other Books in The TAB Furniture Woodshop Series

Designing and Building Colonial and Early American Furniture, with 47 Projects—2nd Edition

Capture the spirit and challenge of authentic Early American and Colonial craftsmanship.

A recognized expert provides first-rate illustrations and simple instructions on the art of reproducing fine furniture. Each piece is accompanied by exploded drawings, detailed materials lists, and plenty of suggestions for project variations. There are complete directions on how to recognize good furniture design, find solutions to specific design problems, use power tools, and more. Every project is an exquisite reproduction of centuries-old originals: a drop-leaf table . . . firehouse armchair . . . peasant chair . . . ladderback chair . . . gateleg table . . . dry sink . . . love seat . . . and other authentic, ''new'' antiques.

Designing and Building Children's Furniture with 61 Projects—2nd Edition

A step-by-step guide to making all kinds of children's furniture and toys, from cribs, cradles, and desks, to a rocking horse, play house, and toy box.

Devoted entirely to children's furniture, this book shows you how to turn inexpensive materials into useful furnishings children will enjoy. You'll learn the basics of furniture making, along with some important woodworking tips and techniques. Packed with two-color illustrations and easy-to-follow instructions, this revised edition provides everything you need to construct useful, sturdy furniture that is as much fun to make as it is to use.

Designing and Building Outdoor Furniture, with 57 Projects—2nd Edition

Build beautiful, sturdy outdoor furniture and patio accessories.

This book is filled with practical, easy-to-understand instructions and detailed two-color illustrations. Even the novice woodworker will be able to make outdoor tables, chairs, benches, planters, and more. Advice is offered on tools, materials, and techniques. Fifty-seven projects are described in detail, from simple benches to a more complicated picnic table.

Designing and Building Space-Saving Furniture, with 28 Projects—2nd Edition

Unique ideas for saving money and space with built-in furniture you create!

Step-by-step directions, exploded drawings, detailed materials lists, and plenty of suggestions for project variations explain every aspect of making space-saving furniture. An excellent guide to designing and constructing built-in furniture, this book provides the novice craftsman with a complete course in measuring, marking, designing, and building furniture to meet specific space restrictions. Projects include complete instructions for building corner and hanging cabinets, room dividers, and units for kitchens, bedrooms, and other household areas.

Do-It-Yourselfer's Guide to
Furniture Repair & Refinishing
2nd Edition

Percy W. Blandford

TAB BOOKS Inc.
Blue Ridge Summit, PA

SECOND EDITION

FIRST PRINTING

Copyright © 1988 by TAB BOOKS Inc.
First edition copyright © 1977 by TAB BOOKS Inc.
Printed in the United States of America

Reproduction or publication of the content in any manner, without express permission of the publisher, is prohibited. No liability is assumed with respect to the use of the information herein.

Library of Congress Cataloging in Publication Data

Blandford, Percy W.
    Do-it-yourselfer's guide to furniture repair and refinishing.

    Includes index.
    1. Furniture—Repairing—Amateurs' manuals.
2. Furniture refinishing—Amateurs' manuals. I. Title.
TT199.B55 1988   684.1'044   88-2243
ISBN 0-8306-0994-6
ISBN 0-8306-2994-7 (pbk.)

Questions regarding the content of this book should be addressed to:

Reader Inquiry Branch
TAB BOOKS Inc.
Blue Ridge Summit, PA 17294-0214

Cover photograph courtesy of Davis Publications, Inc.

Edited by Suzanne L. Cheatle
Designed by Jaclyn Saunders
Illustrations by Grace Meyer

Contents

SECTION II REPAIRING FURNITURE

SECTION III REFINISHING OLD FURNITURE

Introduction

Every day, do-it-yourselfers are rediscovering the traditional furniture-making skills that helped to create the world's finest furniture. The reason is simple: Do-it-yourselfers would rather repair furniture than dump it; they'd rather refinish it than store it; they'd rather create it than buy it.

To the do-it-yourselfer, restoring furniture means creativity, fun and savings. That's what this book is all about. Step-by-step instructions are included here to help you perform just about any repair or refinishing job on any piece of furniture. You might be surprised how easy it is to use professional techniques. Carving, veneering, turning, antiquing, staining, planing—they're all easy to learn, with a little practice, a little patience.

Fortunately, you don't need a lot of expensive equipment, just a few basic tools and learnable skills. With this book, you learn how to make a piece of furniture as beautiful, as well-crafted as it ever was—or better!

Section I
FINISHING
NEW WOOD

Selecting a Finish

NEARLY ALL FURNITURE has been made from wood during the thousands of years that man has had the skill to work with it. Metal, leather, fabrics, and plastics have their place, but wood has character, workability, and durability.

Wood is a natural product that comes from an enormous variety of trees. Different kinds of wood have unique characteristics. The way a softwood is treated might be very different from what is done to a choice piece of hardwood.

The finishes of wood furniture can vary according to what the furniture is used for. A showpiece can have a very different finish from something that will have to stand up to the hard knocks of a playroom.

Different kinds of finishes can do various things. A finish can disguise the appearance of wood or allow the grain to show through. Anyone who has an appreciation for wood will want the furniture to show its beauty as wood, but there are occasions when a more opaque finish would be better.

WHY APPLY A FINISH?

Why apply a finish at all? Wood is a porous material, and pores absorb dirt. It is this problem that makes the application of a finish almost essential. It is possible to leave some wood bare, but then it must be scrubbed periodically. Obviously, this would not do for a choice piece of cabinetwork.

Bare wood can be damaged. Comparatively slight abrasion or hitting can mark it. These marks can only be removed by working away the surface to below the depth of damage. A finish on the surface provides a barrier to this sort of damage. Many finishes are harder or more resilient than wood.

Although the protective aspects of a finish are important, it is appearance that usually settles the choice of finish. Some woods are not attractive in themselves, but a comparatively plain wood with little grain showing can be beautified by the right finish.

STAINING

The color of some woods might be uneven or unattractive. Fortunately, color can be altered by staining. Most staining, though, is a matter of intensifying color, not transforming it. Today very little antique furniture is in its natural color; its new color is usually a deeper shade of the original. Most traditional oak furniture has been stained a darker brown. Nearly all mahogany furniture has been made more red than it was originally.

Sometimes a piece of furniture with exposed parts made of fairly expensive wood might have unexposed parts made from cheap wood stained to match. Staining lets wood grain show through; painting does not. This should be remembered. Plywood, which has its veneers cut around the circumference of a log, usually has a wide wavy grain that is unlike the grain of any other solid wood. And stained plywood looks just like what it is: stained plywood.

Bleaching has the opposite effect of staining. Instead of darkening the wood, it lightens it. Bleaching is sometimes used throughout a construction to get special effects. More often, however, bleaching is a way of lightening certain areas of wood so they match surrounding areas. Sometimes a part is bleached to match the whole construction. In such cases, bleaching of a part might be followed by staining the whole thing.

A good staining enhances the wood grain. So it usually preferable to keep staining light and aim for an even color that lets the character of the wood show through. Most stains soak in and do nothing except color the wood. There are a few, though, that have some body and partially cover or fill the grain. These have their uses for special effects, but in general they should be avoided. They can create a muddy appearance.

Wood is absorbent. Often if a finish is applied directly to bare wood, most of it will soak in. For some finishes a succession of coats applied in this way may be correct, but for many finishes the wood must be sealed, or filled, first. Scaling is particularly important for woods with very open grain. Sometimes even after many applications of a finish to bare wood, the surface is filled with dents where the finishing material has settled into the hollows. Sealing is an easy method of preventing such unevenness.

Most opaque finishes are paint, but there are lacquers and other materials that are also opaque. In recent years, the things used for opaque finishes have changed considerably, mainly because of the introduction of synthetic ingredients.

PAINTING

Some old furniture was painted, although the beauty of natural wood was always appreciated. There was a time when furniture made from good wood was covered with paint, embellished by gilding, and ornamented with artful carvings. At yet another time, the whole surface of a piece of furniture was covered with carvings. Today, however, most painted furniture requires no such trappings.

A painted finish has certain advantages and disadvantages. Wood furniture with a clear finish generally blends easily with other room furnishings, but a painted finish might clash if it is badly chosen. On new work a painted finish might be more appropriate in places where dust and dampness are expected. Paint is also the finish for furniture made from softwood or several different types of wood.

If protection is an important consideration, a gloss paint is usually tougher than a semigloss paint. It is also easier to clean. A glossy finish does not hold dirt the way duller finishes do.

In the past, stains, clear finishes, and paints were prepared by the user, and many craftsmen kept their own trade secrets. Today all these things can be bought ready-made. They are compounded by experts and made up precisely according to formulas. There is, however, a satisfaction in making your own finish, and some are quite simple to make.

In later chapters, you will learn to select and use both traditional and modern finishes.

2

Preparation of Wood

THE SUCCESS OF ANY FINISH is dependent on what goes before. It is important that the final coat be applied properly, but if all the preparatory work has not been done thoroughly, the finish could be a disaster. If the finish is one that will show the grain, proper attention to the surface of the wood, before any treatment is applied, is most important. Even when paint is the final treatment, producing a good finish is much easier if the wood surface has been properly prepared.

BASIC CONSIDERATIONS

Wood is a fibrous material. In some woods the fibers of the grain are easily seen. When wood is worked, ragged fibers are produced. These ragged fibers cause surface roughness. The elimination of this roughness is what wood preparation is all about.

First cuts in wood leave coarse fibers. Sawing leaves a rough surface made up of these fibers. Planing smoothes down the roughness somewhat, but ragged fibers will still remain. Successive smoothing gradually reduces the raggedness until it virtually disappears.

Particularly in repair work, the choice of wood is usually dictated by the need to match something already existing. If the kind of wood used doesn't matter, however, it is usually best to avoid wood with very pronounced grain. Heavily grained wood is more difficult to bring to a smooth, even surface than wood with a less obvious grain. Lightly grained wood is easier to stain too, because it soaks up stain more evenly.

A lot of woods contain resin or oil. Some softwoods have resin pockets, and knots that break the surface might exude resin that can spoil finishes.

Oils in some woods can work to the surface long after the wood has been made into furniture. Teak is one of these woods. Any finish applied to it must take into account the oil. There are oil finishes that bring out the beauty of teak, but some finishes appropriate to other woods would not last on teak.

The first work done on wood is usually sawing. A coarse saw might be used to cut the wood from the log. Usually a finer power saw is used to bring the wood to the size needed for furniture. Using a power saw can be tricky, however. Pushing wood against a circular saw at too high a speed can cause the fibers to tear out. The sawing should be slow and easy, especially if the wood will be planed. Breakouts caused by hasty sawing can be too deep for even a planer to remove without taking the wood below size.

PLANING

Wood that is machine planed often has very obvious ridges across the surface, caused by forcing the wood over the cutters too quickly. Buying machine-planed wood, even if the planing is poor, is better than buying sawn wood, however, because flaws not apparent in a sawn surface might show after planing.

Perfection in the cutters of a planer cannot be maintained. Using sharpened cutters just one time can dull them slightly. Usually this slight dullness doesn't matter, but blunt cutters can cause problems. Blunt cutters pounding a wood surface will case-harden it: they will bend over fibers (instead of slicing them off) and press them into the surface. Later on, possibly not until the application of a liquid finish, those bent fibers can rise and cause roughness.

Sometimes it might be sufficient to follow careful machine planing with sanding. If you need to do prolonged power sanding to get a satisfactory surface, however, there is a risk of bending the fibers instead of cutting them, especially if you use worn abrasive paper or cloth.

For the finest surface, machine planing should be followed by hand planing. If a power planer is unavailable, you may plane the surface with a jack plane, followed by a shooting plane for long edges. A smoothing plane is even better for producing a clean, even surface.

Sharpen the blades of hand planes straight across, but round the blade corners to prevent digging in. The shaving taken off a wood surface should have an even thickness right across. It shouldn't be thicker at the center. Set the mouth of the plane no wider than necessary. Have the cap iron reasonably close to the cutting edge. All these steps contribute to smooth, fine cuts with a minimum risk of surface tearing.

On most woods, you can use the smoothing plane *along* the grain. A first cut will show the way. If the result is not as smooth as expected, turn the wood around and try planing the other way.

Twisting grain, caused by a knot or burr on the tree, is sometimes a desirable feature on wood. If such a grain can be planed at all, it will be *across* the grain. If you have any doubt about the success of planing this sort of surface, it is better to sand.

For most woods, sanding after hand planing will produce a surface good enough to apply a finish to. For some woods, however, it is better to scrape after planing. A properly sharpened scraper has a finer cut than a plane in the best condition. A scraper does not remove much, but it leaves a smoother surface because it cuts off the finest wood fibers. A scraper is a piece of steel with a sharp edge. The old-time cabinetmaker scraped with the edge of a piece of glass.

On most woods, you can use the scraper in any direction in relation to the grain. When you scrape a planed surface, you should go over it systematically. Even those areas that appear to have good surfaces should be scraped. The scraper can be safely used over irregular grain that would tear up under a plane.

If you use plywood with solid wood, it is best to scrape the veneer. Generally, you can improve the appearance of the plywood and make the finish more nearly the same as the adjoining wood if you scrape it all over, even if sanding is to follow. Scraping removes many of the ends of fibers that are in plywood.

If the plywood has been veneered with choice wood, however, the surface might be too thin to withstand scraping, except on obvious irregularities or high spots.

SANDING

All these preceding steps get the wood to a good state so little sanding is needed. Sanding breaks off some minute fibers and bends others. The best finish results from doing no more sanding than is necessary to complete the preparatory processes.

Much old furniture dates from the days before abrasive papers and cloths were made with any degree of precision. The usual grit was sand, which varied according to the rock from which it was produced. The marvelous finish on some antique furniture was produced by tools and had little or no treatment with abrasives.

Sanding Papers

The term *sanding* is a carryover from the distant past. Sand as a grit fell from use a long time ago; the term *sandpaper* as a name for all abrasives is really not accurate.

It is only in comparatively recent times that there has been any standardization of abrasive grades. Even standardized grades are inconsistent, however. The best grading is by the number of grits per square inch. Fifty grits per square inch is very coarse, and 320 is very fine. Fineness continues to 600 grits per square inch or more for very fine abrasives used on metal and fiberglass. Other grading systems use numbers and letters, which have no specific meaning other than the traditional ones and do not necessarily mean the same thing in different grits. TABLE 2-1 gives some approximate comparisons. There are also traditional categories: papers used on bare wood are *cabinet papers*; fine abrasives used to rub down finishes are *finishing papers*.

—————— **Table 2-1.** Abrasive Grades—Approximate Equivalents. ——————

Use	Grits	Traditional	Glasspaper	Emery cloth
Finest (for finishes)	400	10/0 (ten nought)		
	320	9/0		
	280	8/0		
Very fine (for bare wood)	240	7/0		
	220	6/0		
Finest (commonly used on wood)	180	5/0	00 (flour)	0
	150	4/0	0	FF
Medium sanding	120	3/0	1	F
	100	2/0	1 1/2	1
Usual first sanding	80	0	F2 (fine 2)	1 1/2
	60	1/2	M2 (middle 2)	2
Rough sanding	50	1	S2 (strong 2)	3
	40	1		
		1/2	2 1/2	4
	36	2	3	

The next grit used after sand was powdered glass. It is still possible to get glasspaper, but it has been displaced by other grits. A common cheaper grit is flint, made from quartz or silica. Flint tends to wear quickly and clog with dust rapidly, so overall it might not be cheap. For surfaces that would clog in any case though, such as when removing an old finish, flint is worth using.

A good paper for general sanding of wood is one using garnet, a tawny mineral. This paper is fast cutting, with less tendency to clog, and each piece has a reasonable life. Another good paper is made from aluminum oxide, derived from bauxite. It is grayish, fast cutting, and long lasting. It can be used on bare wood, but is particularly useful for rubbing down lacquer and other finishes.

Silicon carbide paper works better on metal and fiberglass, but it can be used on wood. This paper has crystals that are hard, sharp, and irregular, so they cut rapidly. The paper can be soaked in water or other solvent, which is why it is often called *wet-and-dry* paper. Using water allows dust to be flowed away, making for cleaner cutting. This is valuable when rubbing down hard finishes, but there are occasions when this paper can be used on bare wood.

Abrasives come on paper or cloth backing and occasionally on other materials. In the cheaper papers, the grit is held by a nonwaterproof glue. As a result, damp atmosphere can weaken the glue, causing the grit to come loose after a few strokes. Warming the paper first will prevent this problem. Other grits are either fixed to the backing with waterproof adhesive or fused on by other means. Cloth backing is usually more durable than paper and is to be preferred for hand-sanding of curves. Cloth-backed papers are essential for power sanding.

Abrasives are available in bands and disks to suit machines. For hand sanding, however, standard-sized sheets are about 9 × 11 inches. If used folded and freehand, the paper might not last long and the surface might not be as good as expected. For flat surfaces, the paper should be wrapped around a block. It is best if the block has a surface slightly softer than the wood being sanded. The block can be cork, hard rubber, felt, or wood. If it is wood, it should be faced with a sheet of one of the other materials. A facing about 3 × 5 inches will do. There are special sanding blocks with handles and chips to hold the paper, but most workers prefer to hold the paper on by hand. Keep the face of the block clean. A piece of grit between the block and the paper can score the wood, particularly when you are finishing with a fine paper.

Sanders

Power sanders come in three forms: disk sanders, which sand in a circular motion; belt sanders, which use a band of abrasive cloth that moves over a pressure plate, and orbital (oscillating) sanders, which have a flat plate that moves the abrasive sheet rapidly over a small area.

Disk sanders make curved scratches in the work, all of which must be removed by later sanding. They can be used to reduce awkward shapes to size, but they are unsuitable for finishing. A belt sander has limitations, too. It is excellent on narrow strips, but on broad surfaces there is a risk of the edge of the belt causing ridges. For finishing work, the orbital sander is a good choice.

The orbital sander has a vertical motor that operates a rectangular pad, to which flat pieces of abrasive paper can be clipped. Although the actual movement of the pad follows a curve, the sander does not leave visible cross-grain scratches.

Sanding Procedures

Sanding of flat surfaces should normally be *with* the grain. The scratches from the abrasive will be less apparent this way. However, initial sanding may be *diagonal* to the grain, particularly if there is unevenness from planing or other tool work. In any case, final strokes with fine abrasives must be *with* the grain to remove any visible scratches.

When sanding flat surfaces near an edge, be careful not to let the abrasive dip and round the edge, unless you want a rounded edge. Rounding edges unintentionally is very easy to do.

Do not be tempted to revert to planing once you have begun to sand. Deal with all blemishes that need planing *before* you begin sanding. Grit from an abrasive can blunt a plane edge, and plane cuts after sanding are difficult to disguise.

Hand sanding can achieve the same results as power sanding, providing the abrasive used in hand sanding is of a finer grit. Hand sanding with 180-grit paper would produce the same surface as power sanding with 150-grit paper.

When you must sand moldings or other shaped work, it's best to wrap the abrasive paper around a shaped piece of wood or around your finger. The problem with freehand sanding is the risk of rounding where an edge should be left square. You will need to sand corners and angles in shaped work carefully with the edge of a piece of abrasive paper. This job can be tedious, but there's no other way to sand such surfaces.

Abrasive papers are not the only method of sanding. Sanding used to be done with abrasive powder imbedded in cloth or a felt pad. Today you can use this method to rub down finishes between coats. It is also possible to sand with a fine powder, such as pumice or household scouring powder (dry), as a final smoothing after abrasive paper.

Steel wool is also used as an abrasive, but do not use the type sold for domestic scouring. Steel wool comes in grades from 000 (finest) to 3 (coarsest). Grade 1 is the coarsest that you need to use on furniture, and for finishing a wood surface you should use 00 to 000. You can use steel wool in places that are difficult to deal with using abrasive paper. Generally steel wool should be regarded as a final step after sanding. Some woods, particularly oak, can be discolored by the use of steel wool. It is important to remove particles of steel wool from the surface of any wood. A slightly dampened cloth will accomplish this step.

The best way to judge a sanded surface is with your fingertips. Do not try to judge smoothness with your eyesight.

Before you apply a finish, you must remove all dust from the wood surface. A cotton glove or a soft rag will do the job. Remember that the slightest trace of dust—visible or invisible—can mar a finish.

Usually, sanding is quite successful if done with the wood dry, but sometimes a wet surface is best. On some woods, particularly some of the softer and more fibrous woods, fiber ends will bend, even with the sharpest tools and keenest abrasives. The fibers might straighten and spoil the surface when a liquid finish is applied. The best way to prevent at least some of this trouble is to wet the surface between sanding treatments. Moisture will make the bent fibers stand up. Let the wood dry, then sand again.

Sometimes it's best to sand furniture parts before final assembly. They're more accessible then. If all parts are accessible after assembly, it's common practice to wait until the whole thing is together. Sanded parts can take a lot of nicks and scratches while they are being transformed into a single piece of furniture.

There is also a case for sanding shaped parts before they are cut. If the end of a piece of molding abuts a flat surface, sanding it right up to the joint would be difficult in position. It would be better to sand before the joint is cut. If you then make the joint carefully, the finish will extend right into the angle. This also applies to a miter, such as the corner of a frame. Sand the strip of molding in the length before you cut its miter joints.

Round work is often sanded in the lathe. You should finish any turned wood with progressively finer abrasives while in the lathe, but this is not enough. Such sanding is *across* the grain, so it is always advisable to further hand-sand the broader surfaces *with* the grain.

BLEMISHES AND FLAWS

If the wood used and the workmanship are perfect, there is no need for any further treatment of the furniture before it is introduced to the finishing processes. Wood is a natural material, however, and it can have flaws. Faulty craftsmanship can leave blemishes. It is possible, however, to deal with many defects so they are not visible in the finished work.

Some of this attention must be given before sanding begins. Some of it might come intermediately. It might be advisable to do the first sanding and make repairs before further sanding. Some repairs are best delayed until after staining.

A *dent* doesn't mean that wood has been removed; it means that wood has been compressed. Sometimes sanding the area around a dent can bring the whole surface to the same level. Adding water to the dent will expand the squashed wood cells. This expansion is sometimes enough to raise the wood to the correct level. Of course, sanding might be necessary after expansion, but only after the dent has dried out.

Water alone might not always work, particularly with the less absorbent woods. In this case, you should add heat. After dropping on a little water, dip a hot piece of steel in it until steam appears. The steam penetrates where water will not. You might need to repeat the process several times. You might need to treat a bad dent by filling, but it is more satisfactory to raise the wood if possible.

There are several compounds used to fill cracks, joints, knot holes, or sunken nails or screws. These compound are called fillers. Some fillers will not take stain at all, so they must be matched to the wood and used *after* staining. Other fillers absorb stain differently from the surrounding wood, so the resulting shade might be slightly different.

Stick shellac or plastic fillers (sometimes called *beaumontage*) are good for covering sunken nails or small cracks. They do not take stain, however, so you must use them after staining the wood.

Plastic water putty is effective for this purpose. It comes in a powder and is mixed with water to form a thick paste. Press it into cracks or holes with a putty knife, screwdriver, or chisel. Clean off any excess quickly because it sets rapidly. It cannot be softened again with more water, so do not mix more than is needed. Sand the area thoroughly after it has dried. Stray bits of dried putty might show through the finish. If the wood is to be stained, test the stain on the filler before you use the filler on the wood. You can color the filler before mixing by adding colored powder.

Wood compound, a filler paste, is used in the same way as water putty and has similar effects and limitations. It takes about an hour to dry.

When it sets. Plastic Wood (wood plastic) is very much like natural wood. It is made of wood fibers with a plastic binder and comes in tubes, as well as cans. For infrequent use, the tube is best because it excludes air and keeps the contents flexible. As for most fillers, press plastic wood into the wood cavities. It does not contract as it dries, but it is usual to leave a little excess to be sanded off. Let the filler dry about 15 minutes before sanding.

Most fillers just fill gaps; they do not provide much strength. Most glues by themselves cannot fill gaps with any real holding power either. Most glues *craze*, or crack, too easily. The crazing takes away any strength. If sawdust is mixed with glue, however, a strong bonding compound results. You can use this mixture to fill a crack or other exposed flaw, but it is particularly useful for joints that have not pulled close. If you use sawdust from the actual wood, it should make a close match. The glue-sawdust mixture will not take stain, however.

For a painted finish, the color of any stopping or its ability to take stain does not matter. The important thing is a level surface. If softwoods are involved, there is one more requirement. Resin can come through paint long after it has been applied. A barrier must be provided, particularly over knots where the problem is worst. Fortunately a layer of shellac will hold back the resin.

You must remove undesirable dark streaks in wood if you intend to apply a clear finish. Sometimes streaks are less obvious after staining. It's even possible to stain dark areas less to get a more even color.

Bleaching is another way of getting rid of dark areas. Most bleaches can damage your skin, so always use rubber gloves and eye protection when bleaching. Be sure to keep bleaches away from clothing too. Household laundry bleach is a good bleach to use on wood. The best mixture for most applications is 12 parts water and 1 part bleach. Apply the mixture with a cloth until the right wood color is reached. Then wash the surface with water to remove the remaining bleach and allow to dry completely before taking any further step in finishing.

There are commercially produced bleaches for wood, but they are mostly intended for lightening the color all over for special effects. Check the label because some are very potent and might remove too much color.

You also can use oxalic acid for bleaching. It is available from paint stores. Dissolve the crystals in hot water—the amount of water depends on the action required. Two ounces in 1 pint should be strong enough. Apply it hot and use several coats if necessary to get the right color. Then wash it off and allow the surface to dry before continuing the finishing process.

Using bleaches requires more precautions than just wearing rubber gloves and eye protection. Do not use metal containers for mixing bleaches; such containers might affect the action of the solution on wood, even to the point of staining instead of bleaching. To be safe, mix the solution in a glass container. Avoid metal-bound and bristle brushes. Old wood, even if cleaned off, will have its pores contaminated, and bleaching might become patchy or ineffective. If bleach gets on your skin, wash it off with plenty of water and use boric acid to neutralize it.

3

Paint Finishes

IN RECENT YEARS, there have been many changes in the constitution of paints, mainly because of the introduction of synthetic ingredients to replace traditional natural ones. The results have mostly been improvements in quality, but some of these alterations have affected the methods of application. Fortunately, paint manufacturers usually provide a considerable amount of information on their products. It's a good idea to read the instructions accompanying paints because old methods don't always work on new paints.

BASICS OF PAINT

It is best to use a complete paint system produced by one manufacturer. In this way, you can ensure that the various coats and any sealers or fillers will be compatible with each other. Of course, sometimes it is possible to mix paint systems without any complications, but it's best to check the labels. Read the instructions in this chapter in conjunction with the information provided by the paint manufacturer.

The word *paint* generally refers to an opaque finish. When paint is used on wood, the color of the wood and its grain are hidden. Traditionally, paint has been divided into two broad categories: enamel and lacquer. Most enamels dry slowly from the surface down, and they generally produce a relatively soft surface. Lacquers dry quickly and generally produce a hard, polishable surface. An enamel surface usually lasts longer than a lacquered one, which is why most house paints are enamels. Both enamels and lacquers can produce glossy finishes, but a good lacquer can often outdo an enamel in creating a hard, high-shine surface.

Paints come in flat, semigloss, or full-gloss finishes. They cover well and a second coat can follow after overnight drying. Brushes or rollers can be used, and can be cleaned with water. Water-based paint can be used if furniture must match a wall, but the result will be less durable than if ordinary paints were used.

Most do-it-yourselfers don't try to mix their own paint. Any paint shop can supply just about any color you would need. If you insist on mixing your own paint, you should at least get the advice of someone experienced. Most people know that blue and yellow make green, but mixing paints that are already compounds can produce unexpected results. There is also the problem that dried paint might not be the same shade as it is when wet. The color also might be affected by the surface or undercoat below it.

However, if you wish to produce your own colors (instead of mixing existing colors), you should start with white paint. Add color a little at a time and stir thoroughly by hand. Remove all streakiness. At all stages add color slowly. You can always add more, but you cannot take it away after mixing. Remember to check the compatibility of all ingredients.

Two-part paints are generally used on outdoor woodwork and boats. They produce a very hard, waterproof coat that resists saltwater, solvents, and heavy abrasion. These paints are seldom used on indoor furniture, but they are perfect for such things as lawn chairs and bar tops.

Two-part paints consist of resin and an accelerator, or hardener. When the two ingredients are brought together, a chemical reaction takes place and the paint hardens. After the paint has hardened, nothing will reverse the process. Therefore, mix only the paint you will use in a specified time. Any that is mixed and unused will harden and be useless. You must also clean brushes before the hardening process begins.

Most painting jobs on furniture follow this sequence:

☐ Preparation of the surface
☐ Sealing or filling of the surface, if necessary
☐ Application of one or more priming coats of paint that provide a base for other coats
☐ Application of one or more undercoats that provide the base for the last coat
☐ Application of one (or two) top coats that provide the final visible surface

Between some or all of these coats there will be rubbing down to remove irregularities.

Some paints do not require all these steps. Some painting jobs demand only one or two coats, but for the best finish on an important piece of furniture there must be several coats with adequate rubbing down between coats.

With smooth, close-grained wood, it often will be possible to go straight into the use of priming paint. If the wood has a pronounced grain, you might need to sand or fill before painting. Woods like oak have many large pores, which you must fill before painting.

Fillers are used to close the grain and leave a smooth surface on which to paint. Some paint manufacturers provide fillers or sealers for use under their paints. For open-grained wood, the filler should be in paste form. If you need to use a filler on close-grained wood, it can be liquid.

Fillers cannot be made at home; they must be bought ready-made. Some woodworkers thin out paste fillers and brush them on as a first coat. The thinned paste penetrates better. Usually the thinning is done with turpentine or the manufacturer's solvent. Paste filler dries fairly quickly. It can be rubbed with a coarse cloth before it hardens to force filler into the grain and to remove any excess. First rubs should be across the grain. Then change to a soft cloth and wipe gently along the grain until no excess filler is picked up.

A sealer is a coating applied to prevent subsequent coats of material (usually paint) from sinking into the wood. Do not confuse this material with fillers. A sealer is usually applied with a brush, like paint.

Shellac can be used as a sealer; it can prevent resin from oozing through a paint coat. Usually shellac is applied in two coats. The first may be thinned slightly with alcohol to give a better penetration. Then a stronger coat follows. It is applied evenly. Light sanding with a fine abrasive will provide a base for the paint. Chapter 6 gives details of shellac application.

WOOD SURFACES

Fir and other softwood have very open grain. The open grain is even more pronounced in fir plywood because of the way the veneers are cut. After you sand these woods, you should apply a good sealer to them. The sealer creates a flat surface for paint so the grain will not show through. There are sealers especially made for fir. These sealers work very much like a first coat of paint.

You can treat plywood made from hardwoods in the same way as solid woods of the same type. If the wood is close grained, sanding might be all that is needed before the first coat of paint.

Hardboard has a smooth, even surface. Sanding is inadvisable. If the surface is dirty, however, wash it with soap and water. You can remove grease or oil with a degreasing solvent. Unless the hardboard is very solid, though, there is probably no need for treatment before sealing. Use hardboard sealers according to directions. The amount of sealer that hardboard will absorb varies. Some hardboards are very absorbent and might need several coats of sealer. The oil-tempered hardboards have a much greater resistance to absorption and might need little or no sealing. Lightly rub down sealers to produce a smooth surface.

Many modern paint systems do not require priming paint. To a certain extent the terms undercoat and primer are interchangeable. Primer is a fairly thin paint intended to penetrate the fibers of wood to provide a secure drip. An undercoat, in the most general terms, is a coat applied just before the final coat. A primer is the first in the series of coats. If there has been no filling or sealing of a surface, a primer serves, to some extent, as a filler.

Primers tend to be thin, they are usually gray or pink. If they are to be followed by several coats of other paint, their color does not matter.

It is possible to use water-based paint directly on wood as an undercoat. You can apply synthetic or oil-based paint over it. You can put an undercoat directly over the wood or filler. Undercoats cost more than primer and its alternatives, however.

Undercoat paint is always flat to give the top coat a good mat surface to adhere to. The color of an undercoat may be the same or slightly different from that of the top coat. A slight difference in color makes it easier to see how well the final coat covers.

Usually, one top coat is all that is needed. Top coats do not necessarily have to have glossy surfaces. If you use a glossy top coat you must sand it to remove the gloss (after drying) if you intend to apply subsequent top coats. Putting gloss over untreated gloss can result in all kinds of troubles: uneven paint, run, curtains, and blisters.

Sometimes you will need to rub down (sand) a painted surface between coats. You can use fine abrasive paper for a really hard surface, but if the surface powders easily, as it may with primer and undercoats, the abrasive paper must be reasonably coarse to avoid clogging with paint dust. Garnet or other abrasive about 100 grit (2/0) should be about right. On early coats, the sanding can be in all directions, but on later coats most of the sanding should be in the same direction as the brush strokes.

If you will rub down between top coats, it's best to do it with wet-and-dry finishing paper, used wet. Sanding by hand at this stage is important and should be thorough. Remove dust from this sanding with a damp cloth. If the final top coat has imperfections, such as roughness and blemishes, rub down the surface lightly with pumice powder on a damp cloth. As with sanding, this rubbing should be in the same direction as the final brush strokes.

BRUSHING

Applying paint by brush is a fairly simple process, and most people have done it. Using proper techniques, however, always produces noticeably better results.

In the past, paintbrushes were made with natural bristles, bound by metal in a wooden handle. These brushes are still a good choice, but today there are nylon bristles and other alternatives to natural bristle.

Brushes are made in a number of shape and sizes. For normal painting, there are flat brushes, which are graded according to their width. A flat brush is sometimes called a *fitch brush*, and its widths are designated X, XX, or XXX, according to the number of rows of bristle bundles (FIG. 3-1). The larger the brush, the more paint it will hold. Generally, a wide brush is less likely to leave brush marks than a narrower brush; however, the brush size should depend upon the kind of painting to be done. A 2 1/2-inch brush is a good general-purpose one; a 1-inch brush (or narrower) can be used for moldings or intricate work. Brushes come in different thicknesses too.

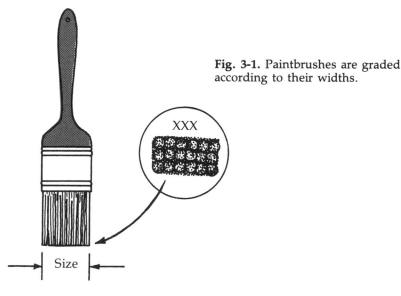

Fig. 3-1. Paintbrushes are graded according to their widths.

Some manufacturers describe their best brushes as varnish brushes, the implication being that only the best is good enough for varnish. A varnish brush is also the best paintbrush, however. You can determine the quality of a brush by manipulating the bristles in your hand. The bristles should be resilient, soft, and even, whether animal bristle or nylon. The ends of animal bristles might be split, which is a good thing. The ends of nylon bristles should be pointed and even. If the brush is described as chisel ended, the bristles are tapered from short to long, like a chisel.

You can extend the life of a new brush by soaking it in linseed oil for about a day. Never stand a brush on its bristles, but hang it so the bristles do not touch the bottom of the container (FIG. 3-2). If the chosen paint is a synthetic that is not compatible with linseed oil, use the solvent recommended by the makers. The object is to soak the bristles and permeate them with the protective oil.

To prepare the brush for use, squeeze or shake out as much oil as possible and wash the bristles in turpentine or paint solvent. Repeat the process several times. Try to get rid of all surplus linseed oil before the brush is used in paint.

Traditionally paint has been stirred before use. With some paints, this procedure is still necessary and advisable, but read the instructions first. Some paints are better left unstirred. If there is a nearly clear film on top of the paint, it must be stirred. If there is a uniform color in the undisturbed paint, it is almost certainly a type that should not be stirred. If it is a paint that should be stirred and it has been standing for a long time, it might be helpful to turn the can over (with a secured lid, of course) for a few hours before you open and stir it. An electric stirrer is speedy, but if there is a considerable amount of very thick paste in the bottom of the can, it might be helpful to disturb this with a stick before using power.

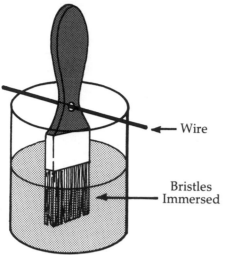

Fig. 3-2. A simple method of suspending a paintbrush in linseed oil.

Wire

Bristles
Immersed

At one time, painters poured new paint into another can or a paint kettle. Today this step is unnecessary. Modern paints can be used directly from the original can. However, wiping excess paint off onto the lip of a can might be messy. One way to avoid the mess is to use a strike wire across the top of the can (FIG. 3-3).

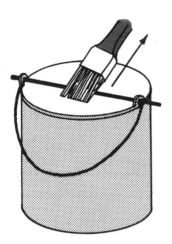

Fig. 3-3. A paint can with a strike wire.

Normally, you should dip only one-third to one-half of the bristle in the paint. Hold the brush with the bristles slightly upwards to minimize dripping and with your first finger and thumb a short distance above the tops of the bristles.

Again, read the instructions. Some synthetic paints cannot take too much brushing. Such paints demand a certain technique. Get the paint on the surface, spread it so it covers evenly, then finish with strokes all the same way. With paint that is not spoiled by excessive brushing, the brush strokes can be in several directions (FIG. 3-4), but the last strokes must be in the same direction.

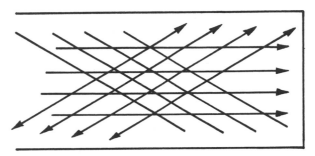

Fig. 3-4. Sometimes paint strokes can be in several directions.

Sometimes the manufacturer's instructions say that the paint should be flowed on. This means that there must be enough brushing to spread it, but once the coat is reasonably even, the paint should be left to find its own level.

If the paint surface includes an edge, work toward it, rather than away from it (FIG. 3-5). Brushing away from an edge can cause dripping (FIG. 3-6).

Fig. 3-5. Paint strokes should be toward an edge, not away from it.

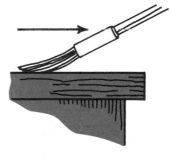

Fig. 3-6. Paint strokes away from an edge can cause dripping.

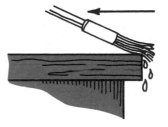

Painting on a horizontal surface is relatively easy. If the furniture can be moved about to bring the working surface horizontal, that is usually advisable. If you must apply paint to a vertical surface, it is usually better to work up and down. Then painting can start at the top, and subsequent brushing can finish with a lifting stroke upward (FIG. 3-7). If the vertical surface is wider than it is high, strokes must be horizontal so that brush marks are lengthwise. Work is still best done from the top, going across the top edge first and working down.

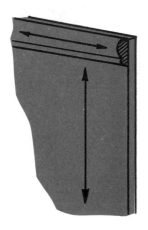

Fig. 3-7. Painting on vertical surfaces should be up and down.

Working on a vertical surface can produce runs or curtains. *Runs* are rivulets of excess paint that slide down the surface; *curtains* are layers of excess paint (FIG. 3-8). Runs and curtains are less likely with up and down strokes, but even then it is important to make sure there is no excess paint left on the surface.

Fig. 3-8. Curtains are the result of excessive paint on the surface.

When you are painting furniture indoors, it is important to keep plenty of light on the surface. A good lamp, as a supplement to regular room lighting, will reveal runs and areas where the paint is too thick.

Most furniture has angular or molded surfaces, as well as flat surfaces. Always paint the shaped parts before you paint the flat parts. You can brush out an excess of paint on nonflat surfaces onto an unpainted flat surface and cover it later.

If necessary, you can use a nearly dry brush to absorb excess paint. You can work out the absorbed paint on scrap wood.

If two different colors are to meet along a line, use masking tape. Paint one color up to the line (or across it) and, after it dries, put masking tape along the line on the painted side. Then you can paint the next color up to the edge of the tape, and it doesn't matter if an unsteady painting hand crosses over onto the tape. Make sure the adhesive of the masking tape will not lift the paint under it. Take up the tape before the second color dries.

Painting should be done in as dust-free an atmosphere as possible. Fortunately, modern paints dry much quicker than traditional paints, but the first few hours after painting are important. Make sure no one can open a door and let in a draft. Consider your own clothes and those of anyone else present. Knitted clothing might harbor dust that can get on the paint. Also, avoid smoking. Some paints are flammable.

Do not be tempted to touch up half-dry paint. The new paint will not bond properly, and it will look bad when it dries. Wait until the paint dries, then sand down any imperfections and try again.

Most factory-made paints seldom need thinning. It is thick paint that causes curtains. If you intend to thin the paint, use only factory-recommended solutions. Turpentine is used in many paints, but some synthetic paints need special thinners. Be very sparing in the amount of thinner you use. Add it in drops; do not pour it. Quite a small amount will thin the paint appreciably. If it is thinned too much, add new paint. Do not thin in the middle of a paint job. The thinning might change the color.

4

Stains and Fillers

STAINS AND FILLERS make wood more attractive. Without them a lot of woods would be nothing more than fireplace fuel. However, the proper use of stains and fillers implies a certain know-how, a certain practical knowledge of staining and filling techniques.

BASICS OF STAINS

Wood does not always need to be stained. Many woods are quite attractive with a clear finish over their natural color. There are, however, several woods that are usually stained to what has been accepted as their normal furniture color. Mahogany usually has its redness emphasized. The brownness of oak and walnut is intensified. To many people, the results are considered the natural color and are accepted as such. Some other woods are normally left in their original color.

Stain is also used when different woods must be matched. The wood of a plywood panel might not be the same color as a surrounding framework, but both can be stained to a similar appearance. Stain can be used to give an inferior wood the appearance of quality. Woods that have an unattractive color can have their appearance enhanced by staining.

Stain should color wood without obscuring its appearance. The details of the grain should show through. Paints and other surface finishes obscure the grain and can be built up to completely hide the base material.

Stains should penetrate the wood. A stain should be applied evenly and smoothly so the finished wood will have an even color. A quick-drying stain might be difficult to get into the wood evenly, but too great a drying time would be inconvenient.

The vehicle of a stain's pigment is the solvent, which carries the color into the pores of the wood. Stains are made with a variety of solvents. A good range of colors can be obtained with each type of solvent, and it is the choice of solvent that mainly concerns the finisher.

OIL STAIN

Oil stain is very popular. Its solvent is a light oil, such as benzene, naphtha, or turpentine. Ready-made stains are available in all quantities and in colors usually described by the name of the wood they are intended to be used on. The actual colors include a variety of browns, reds, yellows, and oranges, as well as a deep black.

Oil stains penetrate well and quickly, but you must allow them at least a day to dry before you apply anything else on top of them. Stains seep through a filler or some other finishes, but you can prevent this problem with a barrier of shellac.

Stains are usually brushed on. Spreading should be with a full brush and with the grain. Lift the brush over the previously applied stain when moving along a surface. Use plenty of stain. The aim is to get the whole surface covered quickly and evenly.

An oil stain will soak in rapidly, and the intensity of color is partly dependent on the soaking time. When the color is right, use a cloth to wipe off surplus stain, stroking in the direction of the grain. Try to allow about the same amount of stain and the same length of soaking time for different sections. Exact timing is not critical, however. With reasonably even brushing and careful wiping, the result should be an even color.

With all stains, it is a good policy to stain the least important parts first and do the important part (usually a top) last. It is helpful to work in a cross light and move the furniture about so the surface being worked on is horizontal, or nearly so, whenever possible.

There might be a problem of uneven absorption. Areas made from sapwood might soak up more than those from heartwood. You can brush extra stain on the heartwood.

In some things, end grain might be a problem. Exposed end grain might soak up stain rapidly so it is considerably darker than other surfaces. Quick wiping of the end grain will minimize this problem, but even then you might not be able to reduce the darkening much. You can reduce the amount of end grain absorption by partial sealing. Apply a coat of thin shellac on the end grain and allow it to soak in and dry before you apply the stain. Be careful that the shellac does not get on any adjoining side grain.

When the stain has dried to a mat surface, it will look slightly darker than it will after a clear gloss finish has been applied. If the result is not dark enough you can apply more stain over the first coat.

The solvents are flammable so you might take the obvious precautions while working. It is also advisable to destroy rags used for wiping. A fire could start by spontaneous combustion if oily cloths accumulate.

WATER STAIN

Oil stains are readily available and convenient to use, but water stains can also penetrate the pores of wood.

Water stain comes in liquids or powders. Powders are dissolved in hot water in proportions indicated by the supplier, but you can vary the intensity of a color by using different strengths. The water is stirred as the powder is poured in, then the mixture is left to cool before use. It can then be bottled and kept almost indefinitely.

A very large range of water stains are available. It is possible to buy certain basic colors and blend your own stain, or buy the powders already compounded to give particular wood colors. You can mix concentrated mixtures to get desired effects, and add water to lighten colors or more stain to darken them.

Water stain leaves a transparent finish that does not affect the appearance of the wood. Drying time depends on temperature and humidity, but a few hours should be sufficient. One problem with the use of water stain is the raising of the grain, as mentioned in Chapter 2. Water stain has the same effect as treating the wood with water, but it would be unsatisfactory to rub down with abrasive paper after staining because this would affect the appearance of the stained wood. Wet the wood with clear water, allow it to dry, and then sand it. Remove sanding dust, then apply the stain.

Water stain is brushed on. There is some advantage in having a stiff brush. Use plenty of stain and brush along the grain. It is a help in getting even coverage to apply two coats of a lighter stain, rather than one coat of a dark stain. Excess water stain splashed onto plain wood is not as easy to disguise as oil stain. It is best to do the whole staining of a piece of furniture as quickly as possible. Usually, you will not wipe with a cloth. You can lift excess stain from corners or moldings with a dry brush.

SPIRIT STAIN

Special colored powders are dissolved in spirits (alcohol) to make stain. Spirit stains do not come in a large range of colors, but there are some that are not usually associated with wood shades, such as blue, green, and yellow, which are used for special effect. As with water stains, colors can be blended. The stains are available as powders, which dissolve easily. Concentrated mixtures can be made and thinned for use.

With alcohol as a solvent, penetration is quick, although not always deep. With near instantaneous drying, it is almost impossible to stain a large area and avoid brush marks. Consequently, spirit stain is not really a general-purpose one for large pieces of furniture. An exception is when spraying is possible—then an even effect is more easily obtained.

Spirit stain is suitable for small items, where overlapped brushing (which causes streaking) does not occur. Moldings for picture frames and similar items can be spirit-stained. Spirit stain is also useful for touching up. It can be used where other stains have been used, and even over many finishes.

Brushing with spirit stains should be done rapidly. Keep the brush moving. Spread the stain with sweeps, but do not try to stretch the stain. Refill the brush as needed and try to always follow a wet edge, rather than a dry one.

It is possible to continue with other finishing processes almost immediately after applying spirit stain, so there is an advantage when the work must be completed quickly. The difficulty of getting an even color on a large surface means that spirit stain is not the choice for a large area. Also, some of the colors fade easier than water and oil stains.

OTHER STAINS

It is possible to use other solvents for stains, but oil and water are the usual choices. Some staining is done with diluted paint. This may be described as pigmented oil stain. The coloring matter is a pigment, which does not dissolve. Consequently, the result is not as transparent as other stains. It is brushed on and wiped off. Because its penetration is slight, you can lighten its color by wiping with a solvent, usually turpentine. In the treatment of new furniture, there is little use for pigmented oil stain, but it has uses in treating antique furniture or faking furniture to look old.

CHEMICAL COLORING

It is possible to alter the color of wood with chemicals. What can be done depends on the particular wood. What has an effect on one wood might be ineffective on another. The final color is a result of a chemical reaction. Some of the chemicals used are caustic, so wear rubber gloves and old clothing.

You can give oak and chestnut a deep brown color with ammonia. Brush on the ammonia in a well-ventilated area. Chestnut and oak are the only woods suitable for this treatment, but the quality of the warm brown color achieved is different from anything obtainable with liquid stains.

Another way of turning many woods a medium brown is to use permanganate of potash. This is bought as crystals to dissolve in water. The resulting mixture is safe to handle and use.

BASICS OF FILLERS

On many woods, filling is necessary to seal the tiny cells in the surface and the much larger visible hollows. Without filling, the finish would sink into the hollows and holes, revealing an unevenness on the surface. Some fillers applicable to painting have been described in Chapter 3. The color of a filler to be used under paint is unimportant, but when a clear finish is to follow, the color of the material used is vital. Fillers are broadly divided into paste fillers, for open-grained woods; and liquid fillers, for close-grained wood.

If the filler can absorb stain at the same rate as the wood fibers, the filler can be used before the wood is stained. In most cases, it is better to do the staining first so the stain will achieve maximum penetration without any filler in the wood to restrict its progress. The filler's color, of course, must match that of the stain.

The filling material itself is a fine powder. The powder in most newer fillers is a finely ground silica, called Silex. The Silex can be formed into a paste with linseed oil or other binder. A liquid sealer can be created by thinning this paste.

Not all woods can be classified as open or close grained. For intermediate types, a paste filler will need to be diluted slightly. TABLE 4-1 lists filler requirements of several woods.

_____Table 4-1. Requirements of Some Woods._____

Paste Filler	Medium Filler	Liquid Filler	No Filler
Ash	Butternut	Bass	Aspen
Chestnut	Korina	Beech	Cypress
Elm	Mahogany	Birch	Ebony
Hickory	Rosewood	Cedar	Gaboon
Lacewood	Sapele	Fir	Hemlock
Oak	Tigerwood	Gum	Holly
Padouk	Walnut	Maple	Magnolia
Teak		Poplar	Pine
		Sycamore	Redwood
			Spruce

PASTE FILLERS

Paste fillers come in many wood colors. In choosing a filler, let it be slightly darker, rather than lighter, than the stain because fillers tend to dry lighter. If you are mixing paste fillers, prepare enough for the whole job in one mix and make sure there are no streaks or unmixed colors in the batch. It is difficult to get the exact color again if more must be mixed.

If a filler needs thinning for brush application, use benzene. Thin it just enough to make brush spreading possible. You can apply paste filler with a cloth, and some woodworkers favor an old hair brush or something similar.

If oil stain has been used, it is advisable to spread on a thin coat of shellac before filling. With bare wood or other stains, however, you can apply the filler without other preparation. Try to spread the filler evenly. Leave it long enough to allow the surface to dull. Rub over the surface with a piece of coarse cloth, first across the grain to force the filler into the grain. Change to a soft cloth and wipe along the grain until all excess filler has been removed.

Coarse cloth might not go into the corners and hollows of shaped parts. A short-haired stiff brush will do the job, though. Filler left on the surface will spoil the subsequent finish, so it is important to remove all filler that is not actually in the pores of the wood. If the filler gets too hard to wipe off properly, dampen it with a cloth soaked in benzene. If you are not sure that all the pores are filled, you can apply a second application of filler without affecting the first application. Although filler might dry in a short time, allow the filled surface to dry a day before you move on to the next treatment.

LIQUID FILLERS

You can transform paste filler into liquid filler by diluting it with benzene or turpentine. Liquid filler is brushed on and wiped after dulling.

Shellac can be used as a liquid filler. It is brushed on, allowed to dry, then lightly sanded. This process is repeated at least once. There are white and orange shellacs. White suits light finishes, but orange can go over darker stains. Use varnish as a filler only when the finish is to be varnished.

Of course, a lot depends on the wood. Some woods do not require fillers—liquid or otherwise.

5

Varnishes

VARNISH CAN BE THOUGHT OF as a paint without color. Varnishes have been used for thousands of years to give wood a clear, glossy finish. For all but the last half century, varnishes have consisted of natural resins and *lacs*, a natural oil vehicle, thinner, and a drier. In recent years, some of these natural materials have been replaced with synthetic ones. Although some natural varnishes might still be obtainable, the newer types are superior in many ways.

BASICS OF VARNISH

Varnish can provide protection for outdoor woodwork and has been used on boats. It is not usually sprayed. Its finish is something like brushed shellac, but it is more durable and better able to resist attack by solvents and heavy objects.

The new synthetic varnishes include vinyl coatings, alkyd-based varnishes, phenolic varnishes, and polyurethanes. The most popular for indoor furniture is polyurethane, and for outdoor phenolic varnish. Your local retailer can give you the brand names and comparative benefits of these products.

Regular varnishes, whether synthetic or natural, are single solution. There are two-part varnishes, however. After the two parts are mixed, there is a limited working time, during which the varnish must be applied. After that the varnish hardens fairly quickly, but builds up a greater hardness over a few days. It is then very hard—even resisting some abrasives. It can even be polished with metal polish. It is fully waterproof and will resist several liquids that would attack other varnishes or paint.

APPLICATION

These notes apply to the use of synthetic varnish. Some additional notes applicable to natural resin varnish are at the end of this chapter.

Although modern varnish becomes dustproof in about 2 hours, the work area should be as dust-free as possible. Guard against drafts. Vacuum-clean just before starting work. Some flow of air is necessary, but arrange it so there is no violent draft near the work.

Varnish is influenced by temperature. Although modern varnishes can be applied in a large range of temperatures, anything less than 65°F causes varnish to flow sluggishly. If the temperature is over about 85°F, varnish might get too liquid. If the work must be done in cold conditions, it is helpful to warm the wood slightly and have the can of varnish standing in hot water (FIG. 5-1). Maintain the room, varnish, and wood at about 70°F for ideal conditions. Avoid extreme temperatures when storing varnish.

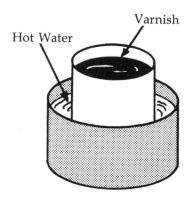

Varnish

Hot Water

Fig. 5-1. A method of softening cold varnish.

Be thorough in your preparation of the wood. Grease and dirt interfere with the way the varnish behaves after it is applied, so see that the wood is kept clean.

When it comes to varnishing, brushes are very important. Brushes must be clean and should be used for varnishing only. Despite the greatest care in cleaning, some contamination from painting could be left in the brush and this would affect the varnishing. Shake or knock out dust from a new brush; then wash it in solvent and dry it.

Most synthetic varnishes should not be stirred. Even a small amount of stirring can introduce bubbles, which might not disappear until they break on the wood surface, leaving tiny blemishes. Handle the can carefully. Shaking it or dropping it before use also might cause annoying bubbles.

Some varnishes should be flowed on. This means using a minimum amount of brushing. Too much brushing also causes bubbles. Brush with the grain. Do not continue after the paint is exhausted from the brush. Do not be tempted to go back over the surface again for another smoothing with an exhausted brush. This action might lift the varnish instead of smoothing it. With paint this step is possible; with varnish, it is inadvisable.

If you are varnishing bare wood, thin the first coat with the thinners or solvent recommended by the manufacturers. This helps the first coat penetrate the wood and bond to it. The amount of thinning depends on the porosity of the wood, but quite a small amount of solvent should be sufficient. Never use shellac as a filler or primer under varnish.

A first coat might raise the grain, flipping up tiny wood fibers into the varnish, even if the wood was prepared carefully. Give this coat a thorough sanding to remove these fibers, but not so much as to go through to bare wood. The grade of abrasive paper will depend on circumstances, but 300 to 500 wet-and-dry should be satisfactory.

Clean the surface of dust after sanding. Apply the next coat unthinned. The number of coats will depend on the desired result. Three is the minimum for a worthwhile finish, and there might be four or five. Rub down along the grain between coats to remove the gloss. Drying time between coats will vary, but it is usually between 12 and 24 hours. Trying to rub down too early will mar the semihard surface. If this happens, or if runs or other flaws occur, wait until the trouble spot is hard and sand it flush, ready to varnish again.

Some manufacturers specify a maximum, as well as a minimum, time between coats. The maximum time is when gloss may be put directly on top of gloss without rubbing down intermediately. For cabinetwork, though, it is best to rub down each coat to get the best finish. Extra coats can always be added to varnish at any time, providing the old coat is clean and rubbed down.

It is unlikely that the top coat will finish absolutely smooth, with an even gloss and without minute blemishes. When it has hardened several days, you can rub it down with pumice powder mixed in either water or light oil on a soft cloth. Rub hard enough to remove flaws and even the gloss, but work gently. Then wipe the surface clean.

No varnish will adhere to a damp surface or to an earlier coat that has not fully dried. Imperfections will show in the surface, and sanding will cause the varnish to pull and break up, instead of smoothing out.

The general technique of varnishing is similar to painting. It is advisable to do parts of least importance first and work toward the more important surfaces. So far as possible, the surface being worked on should be horizontal, and it is helpful to have a light shining across the surface so you gauge progress. Intricate parts are best varnished before adjoining level surfaces so excess varnish is more easily dispersed.

If you are using a natural oil varnish, all of the previous instructions apply, but there are some other points to note. It is possible to brush out a traditional varnish more, so you can work in all directions, providing the final strokes are along the grain. Drying time is longer, at least 24 hours, so the period in which the surface can be affected by dust is longer, probably 12 hours.

Traditional varnish is even more affected by heating fumes than synthetic varnish. Atmospheric conditions are also more important. If there is too much humidity, the varnish might dry with a cloudy effect, called *bloom*. The surface might not dry completely. Temperature is important. Regard 65°F as the minimum. Applying traditional varnish below the minimum temperature might result in incomplete drying.

STORAGE AND CLEANING

For storing, suspend varnish brushes in varnish. Because varnish will oxidize and form a skin on the surface if left in an open container, it is better to completely enclose the brushes in a container with a lid (FIG. 5-2). As with paintbrushes, arrange varnish brushes so their bristles do not touch the bottom of the container. There can be some thinners in the varnish, but the bulk of the liquid should be varnish of the same type the brush has been used with. You can clean a varnish brush in the same way as a paintbrush.

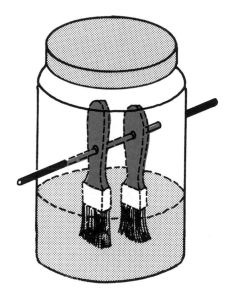

Fig. 5-2. Storing varnish brushes in a sealed container.

6

Shellac

SHELLAC HAS BEEN USED as a wood finish for a very long time. Much antique furniture was finished by French polishing, which is one method of applying shellac. For many centuries, shellac has been used for finishing good-quality furniture. It produced a mellow beauty and even sheen that could not be obtained by any of the other means. Modern materials have taken its place for many applications, but shellac is still used for professional and amateur wood finishing jobs.

BASICS OF SHELLAC

Most shellac comes from India and adjoining regions, where the lac is exuded by an insect that lives on trees. The lac eventually surrounds the insect, killing it in the lac shell that forms. This lac shell is gathered, heated, and stretched into sheets, which are crushed into flakes. Shellac is imported in this flake form.

Shellac dissolves readily in denatured alcohol (methyl alcohol, methylated spirits). Shellac can be bought in liquid form with varying concentrations. The merchant may describe the proportion of shellac to alcohol as a *cut*. The strongest concentration is usually a 5-pound cut, which means that 5 pounds of shellac has been dissolved in 1 gallon of alcohol. There are weaker cuts, down to 2 pounds or lower. Obviously, any concentration might be diluted, but it would be troublesome to add shellac to a weak concentration to make it stronger. So it is better to buy the stronger cut when varying needs are anticipated and dilute with alcohol when a weaker cut must be used.

The normal type of shellac, whether in flake or liquid form, has a transparent orange color. Applying this shellac to wood affects the wood's color slightly, but it works very well on darker woods and can be applied over just about any stain. For lighter colored woods, or those treated by bleaching, there is a white shellac, which is made by bleaching orange shellac. It is not absolutely colorless, but its tint is not obvious on the wood.

Unfortunately, bleached shellac does not have a very long storage life, and it is affected by dampness, which clouds its tint. Normal orange shellac keeps better and has a better resistance to moisture, but it does not stand up to heat, moisture, and most solvents, as well as lacquer and other modern finishes. So orange shellac is not the finish for table and bar tops.

Store shellac in bottles or jars. Do not use metal containers, and do not leave shellac in uncovered containers because the alcohol will quickly evaporate. Do not mix white and orange shellac, and don't use anything but alcohol for thinning.

Spirit stain can be mixed with shellac to produce something similar to varnish stain. This mixture can be used inside a box or other enclosed part, where one-coat stain and finish saves time, but it is not a treatment for an exposed part because the stain is in the shellac coat and not in the wood.

For sealing wood, shellac should be thin—a 2- or 3-pound cut will do. The alcohol in thin cuts takes the shellac into the pores, then evaporates to leave the shellac to a good depth. A thicker concentration might stay mostly on the surface, needing more rubbing down. If left too thick on the wood, shellac might craze and spoil the finish put over it.

BRUSHING

Shellac applied by brush gives an effect comparable to varnish, but shellac does not have as good a resistance to abrasion and many solvents as varnish does. Many coats are needed, but because drying time is short, they can be applied at intervals of 2 hours or so. So three to six coats can be built up in a comparatively short time.

Generally, the best results are obtained with five or six coats of a thin-cut shellac, rather than just a few coats of a stronger shellac. Apply with a broad brush (3 inches for a large surface) and work *with* the grain. Work as quickly as possible. Do not brush excessively and go the whole length in one stroke if possible. Avoid working over a part several times; the quick-drying finish might drag on the brush and spoil the surface. If you do not see a sag or other blemish until it has partly dried, it is better to leave it to sand later. If the blemish is still liquid, work very lightly with just the tips of the bristles.

When brushing shellac on carvings, turnings, and other shaped parts, work quickly. Take care to get into the recesses. Lift away any excess shellac with a dry brush.

Shellac does not perform well in damp conditions, so work in a dry atmosphere. A shellac coat becomes dustproof in only a few minutes.

Allow a little more drying time for the first coat than for later coats. After each intermediate coat dries, sand lightly with a finishing paper. After each sanding, go over the surface and remove dust with a cloth moistened with alcohol. Hard shellac sands as a white powder. If it does not, this is a sign that sanding has started too early.

Shellac will harden in the brush, so between coats put the brush in alcohol. Clean it with alcohol after use.

After you have applied the final coat, there will be a good casing of shellac over the wood, but the surface might not be as smooth as desired. You can rub the surface smooth with a fine steel wool. Rub with long strokes *with* the grain. Avoid circular or cross-grain rubbing and do not apply much pressure. Stop when the surface appears smooth. Follow with a wax polish.

FRENCH POLISHING

The glowing surface obtained by French polishing is considered superior to just about any other gloss finish, but there is more labor involved. Although skill improves with practice, it is patience as much as skill that gets good results. For many items of furniture, any other finish might be just as acceptable as French polishing. If the finish is to go on antique furniture, however, French polish is the correct choice in nearly every case. A great many pieces of furniture now considered antiques were originally French-polished.

Usually French polishing is done with thin shellac. There are mixtures on the market called French polishes, but they are likely to be 2 1/2-pound cut shellacs. Some denatured alcohol contains resin, which makes a less satisfactory polish, so get shellac mixed with alcohol that is free from resin.

Some woodworkers favor additives that they claim improve the finish. Two are gum arabic and gum opal. They are added in very small amounts—not more than 1 teaspoon to 1 pint of French polish (or thin shellac). They are stirred in and left to sit at least half a day before using.

With nearly all woods, French polish is used without coloring. Normally, any coloring comes from staining, before polishing. If, however, you want something different from the orange or white shellac color to match another part, you can mix small quantities of spirit stain with the polish.

French polishing is done with a pad, usually cotton wrapped in a piece of old cotton cloth. The cloth must be free of lint. This pad should be a size that is convenient to handle. The inner cotton should be about 2 or 3 inches across, so the outside cloth needs to be about 9 inches square (FIG. 6-1). To make the pad, bring the cloth up around the cotton and twist (FIG. 6-2). To prevent pads from hardening, store in an airtight jar.

There are three stages in French polishing: bodying in, building up, and spiriting out. Of course, the wood must be brought to a good surface, as described earlier, then stained and filled. If anything, French polishing emphasizes the quality of the wood surface. It is not a finish for disguising imperfections.

Fig. 6-1. A polishing pad's cloth should be about 9 inches square.

Fig. 6-2. The cloth of a polishing pad should be twisted around the cotton.

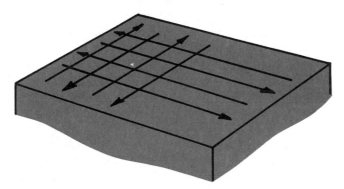

Fig. 6-3. The first rubbing strokes of the bodying-in stage should be across the grain and then with it.

Bodying in is the process that puts a skin of shellac on the wood. Sprinkle shellac on the inner pad and cover it with the cloth. Twist the cloth up so the shellac oozes through. Rub across the grain and then with it (FIG. 6-3). cover every part of the surface, particularly the corners. Do not stop on the surface. Change to a circular motion or a figure-eight action (FIG. 6- 4). Continue rubbing until all the polish in the pad is exhausted. Allow the surface to harden, then recharge the pad and repeat.

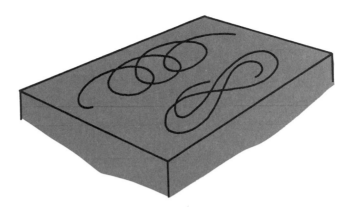

Fig. 6-4. After linear strokes, circular or figure-eight strokes should follow.

Try to cover the whole surface with an even film. It is the corners that suffer. Usually if you concentrate on the corners, the center of a panel will take care of itself. Recharging and rubbing may be repeated as many times as needed to give the whole surface a good protective coating. Leave the work in a dust-free room for about a day.

Follow this step by examining the surface in a light. There might be unevenness. Use fine steel wool lightly to remove this unevenness, then charge the pad and apply more polish. If the pad sticks when you move it over the surface, add a few drops of linseed oil to the outside of the pad. Get an even depth of polish, then wait for another day. If flaws are still there, repeat the rubbing and waiting process.

The *building-up* stage is next. Lightly rub the surface with steel wool and wipe off the dust. Prepare the pad with polish, but not as much as for bodying in. The smaller amount of polish will cause the pad to drag, and you must prevent this problem with a few drops of oil. Do not use any more oil than necessary. To check the pad, press it on paper. Oil will make a mark if present. If none is shown, add a few more drops of oil.

The same test will show how wet the pad is with polish. If there is a definite wet trail when the pad is drawn lightly across the bodied-in surface, there is too much polish on the pad. If the pad marks are shiny, there is too much oil.

Work over the surface with circular or figure-eight movements in the same way as when bodying in. Stroke lightly. Do not rub hard. Make sure the whole area is covered. Do not put down or take up the pad from the center of the surface. Slide on or off at an edge. Do not stop on the surface. It is not swift rubbing that produces a good polish. There's no need to rush.

Recharge with polish as necessary and add spots of oil when needed. Continue until there is a good layer of polish over the surface of the wood.

The layer need not have much of a shine or very even gloss. Next, apply a coat of polish diluted with an equal quantity of alcohol. The result might look smeary, but it does not matter at this stage. Leave the work for at least 5 hours.

The next stage is *spiriting out*. Use a fresh pad with a double outer cloth. Dampen it with a little alcohol. Put the pad into an airtight jar for a short time so the alcohol permeates the pad. Wipe the surface with very light strokes to remove smears. Change to a dry, clean pad and go over the whole surface, first with circular strokes and then *with* the grain. This brushing action should bring up an even glow to the surface. Be careful not to use too much alcohol, which would dissolve too much of the surface that has been applied. Allow the polished work to set for two or three days to fully harden.

French polishing is a process for dealing with large areas. There are many fretted, carved, or molded parts that cannot be treated with a pad. You can rub simple molding lengthwise, but you will need to use a brush to apply shellac to most other shaped parts, even if you polish adjoining flat surfaces with a pad.

7

Spray Finishes

THE SPRAY GUN offers an alternative way of applying a finish to furniture. Although some older finishing materials can be sprayed, lacquer is the most popular sprayed-on finish.

BASICS OF SPRAY FINISHES

Professional spraying equipment is comparatively bulky. The spray gun can be held in the hand, but the gun is connected by a hose to a compressor (usually electrically powered) that is big enough to serve the equipment. Another type uses an electric vibrator in the spray unit. An aerosol can is a simple spray unit, but aerosol spraying should be regarded only as a means of touching up or dealing with small objects.

The simpler spray guns will only take very watery liquids. The better spray units, however, can cope with liquids with more body to them.

When you are spraying, space is an important factor. It is necessary to be able to get around the work, and spray painting in a small enclosed area is never a good idea.

There are two main types of spray guns. In a suction-feed gun, air blows over the outlet, picking up the liquid and atomizing it. In this type of gun, the air and fluid are mixed outside the unit (FIG. 7-1), so it is described as an external mix. In a pressure-feed gun, the fluid is under pressure and there is an internal mix of air and fluid inside the nozzle (FIG. 7-2).

Only a pressure-feed gun can spray heavy liquids such as paint and enamel. Pressure-feed guns are, however, less suitable for fast-drying liquids such as lacquer, which is better sprayed with a suction-feed gun. Many suction-feed guns take glass jars, which are quickly changed. The pressure-feed gun has a metal container.

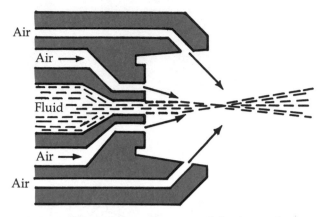

Fig. 7-1. Suction-feed spray guns mix air and fluid outside the nozzle.

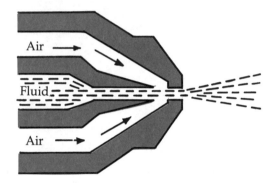

Fig. 7-2. Pressure-feed spray guns mix the fluid and air internally.

The solvents used in some sprays can be uncomfortable—even dangerous—when breathed. Most sprays are flammable, so spraying should be done in a well-ventilated place, preferably with a fan working. Use eye protectors and a mouth mask. It is useful to have a turntable for the work so you do not need to move around a piece of furniture.

LACQUER

The main reason for the popularity of spray finishing is the fast-drying lacquer formulated to give a quick finish and a surface that is highly resilient. Modern lacquer is a complex chemical composition, and should be obtained already mixed. Lacquer is not a mixture to make yourself.

Lacquers are formulated for a variety of purposes, and care is needed to get the right type of lacquer intended for furniture. For most purposes, there is a clear gloss furniture lacquer, but there is a water-white version for use on very light or bleached woods, as well as a flat furniture lacquer. For wood not previously sealed, there is a lacquer sealer to be used before the finishing lacquer.

There are colored lacquers too. These finishes are comparable to brush-painted finishes. Sprayed-on lacquers do not leave brush marks, however. Lacquers usually produce a tougher skin than most paints. Several special lacquers are also made, including a shading lacquer which is used to give shading around edges.

Lacquer will attack other finishes, usually by softening them, so do not spray lacquer over any other finish.

Spraying lacquer usually demands a supply of lacquer thinners, and sometimes retarders are needed. These mixtures are slow drying and prevent the problem of blushing (becoming cloudy white), which might occur in humid conditions.

Lacquer usually must be thinned for spraying. The degree of thinning depends on the manufacturer's recommendations, but a pigmented lacquer will need more thinning than a clear one.

OTHER SPRAY FINISHES

Shellac should be thinned sufficiently to spray smoothly, to a 2-pound cut or thinner. Avoid spraying shellac in humid conditions.

Water-mixed paints can be used with a pressure-feed gun. Thin them with water to a consistency that will spray, but no thinner than the gun will handle.

Synthetic paints vary in their ingredients, and you might need to experiment to discover if thinning is necessary. For the best finish, you will need pause for drying between coats in the same way as when brushing. Some synthetics will work in a suction-feed gun, but all oil-mixed paints need a pressure gun.

Varnishes behave like synthetic paint and might require some thinning. You will need to allow each coat to dry.

Stains can be sprayed too, but the best penetration is obtained by brushing. With stains that are quick-drying and therefore likely to show brush marks, however, spraying should get a more even effect.

SPRAYING

Nothing must block the jet of a spray gun. Therefore, any pigment must be completely mixed in the vehicle, and this mixture must be thoroughly mixed with the solvent or thinner for spraying. Thin as recommended by the manufacturers, but ensure that the result is a free-flowing mixture with the same consistency throughout. If there is any doubt, strain through a fine mesh screen or nylon stocking.

Test-spray on a piece of cardboard or paper so you can make any adjustments before you spray the actual job. See that the mixture of air and fluid is atomizing correctly. Experiment with distance and note the pattern produced. Try vertical and horizontal spraying. Adjust the fluid flow to give a small pattern, and try to get even spread, then enlarge the pattern.

For most liquids, the distance from the gun to the surface should be between 6 and 10 inches. When the gun is close, more liquid is deposited on the surface. The more liquid deposited, the faster the gun must be moved to prevent buildup. If the gun is too far from the work, the deposit of liquid will be too slow.

When you are spraying a flat surface, use a parallel action with the gun. Swinging in an arc is a common fault and results in an uneven spread (FIG. 7-3). The gun should start moving before the trigger is pulled, and the trigger should be released before the gun has finished moving.

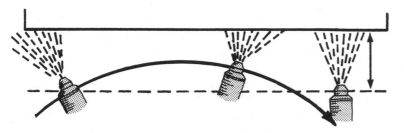

Fig. 7-3. Sweeping the spray gun in an arc can cause unevenness and runs.

To cover an area, let the strokes overlap about halfway so each band gets a double thickness (FIG. 7-4). Where a panel finishes at an edge, spray a band along the edge before doing the lengthwise bands. Treat outside corners in this way, too, with part of the band covering on each surface (FIG. 7-5). With a right-angled corner, it is difficult to avoid over spraying some part, but try to spray each surface separately, with a minimum overlap around the corner. Spraying directly into a corner might cause an excess of fluid in the angle.

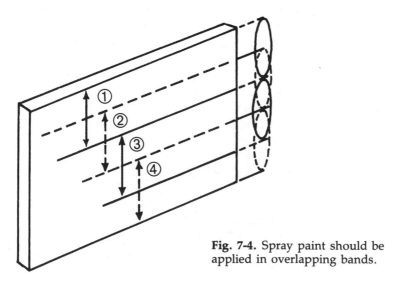

Fig. 7-4. Spray paint should be applied in overlapping bands.

Fig. 7-5. One method of spraying a corner.

For a vertical panel, you can spray with either up and down motions or by horizontal bands. There are no problems like the risk of marks showing after brushing, so the direction of working is not important. What is important is an even coating.

On some items, spraying might be limited to a few parts. As a result, you must mask the part not to be sprayed, but masking tape is not enough. You must join newspaper or cardboard to the masking tape to catch any overspray.

You should think out the spraying sequence before you begin spraying. In general, work from the least important to the most important areas. Spray the insides of cabinets before the outsides. Spray undersides and parts not normally visible. With legs, spray inside surfaces before the outsides. Spray edges before flat surfaces. Leave tops until last. When spraying a surface that adjoins one already sprayed, angle the gun so any spray that overshoots goes into the air over the edge and not around the corner. Although lacquer dries very quickly, you should let furniture sit for 2 hours before you rub down and apply another coat.

SPRAYING FAULTS

Sags or runs are the result of an excess of fluid, usually on a vertical or sloping surface. They might be due to holding the gun still, not releasing the trigger before stopping, working too slowly, or getting too close.

Streaks are caused by uneven spraying. Unevenness can be caused by the gun being held at different distances or erratic overlapping. A sprayed surface can take on a texture like an orange peel if the liquid has not been thinned enough or there is insufficient air pressure. Overspraying on a previously sprayed surface can also cause this problem.

Blooming, or *blushing*, is caused by the absorption of moisture in the finish and occurs when you are working in damp or humid conditions. It could also be a result of lacquer drying too quickly, which you can prevent by adding retarder.

Pin holes, which appear in the finish, are probably caused by the lacquer not being thinned properly. Having the gun too close to the surface or the fluid pressure too high can also cause a pin-hole effect.

Defects in the pattern sprayed are likely to be a result of particle blockages in the gun. Cleaning the gun will remove them. The cause also might be incorrectly mixed material or lack of filtering.

CLEANING A SPRAY GUN

It is important to clean a spray gun soon after use, particularly if you use a quick-drying finish. Do not give the material a chance to harden in the gun. Have an extra container filled with a solvent of the thinner that goes with the material being sprayed.

With the air pressure off, let the fluid tube drip. Work the trigger to release trapped fluid. Wipe off any surplus. Operate the gun when it is filled with solvent. Give several brief squirts. Then seal the nozzle with a cloth and give the trigger a few quick pulls to agitate the solvent in the container and tube. Remove the gauge and squirt again. Remove the solvent container and operate the gun again to blow out any remaining solvent.

If a container needs cleaning, use thinner and a small brush, such as an old toothbrush. If other parts of the gun need cleaning, be careful not to damage air and fluid holes in the nozzle. Do not be tempted to poke through holes with a metal wire or pin. Poking around these areas is better done with a pointed piece of wood or a bristle taken from a broom. If you use water to clean water-based paint, follow by using turpentine or lacquer thinner to reduce the risk of rusting.

Many faults in a sprayed surface can be attributed to a blocked or dirty spray gun or to improperly prepared finishes. It is important that preparation and cleaning be done thoroughly. It is false economy to skimp on thinners or solvents used for cleaning.

8

Oil and
Wax Polishes

IT IS REMARKABLE that some furniture that has survived for hundreds of years still has a fine polish, a mellow patina. The ages seem to have enhanced the fine sheen. Such beauty is the result of expert craftsmanship, and either wax or oil polishes.

OIL POLISHING

Oil polishing takes a lot of time. For this reason, many people avoid it, preferring to use other methods. Oil polishing does, however, produce beautiful finishes.

Many oils can be used, but the most common are tung oil and linseed oil. It is possible to produce a finish on bare wood that is comparable to the finish on old furniture. The oil is spread on, then polished off by vigorous rubbing with one or more cloths. Since most of the oil applied is rubbed off and only a thin film is left in the pores of the wood, the building up of a sheen takes many applications at intervals. Warming the oil by standing its container in hot water aids penetration of the oil. A good oil finish is unlikely to mark by heat or water.

You can begin polishing with coarse cloth. Rubbing must be hard and kept up for some time—as much as 20 minutes. An alternative to the cloth is a stiff scrubbing brush. Cloth wrapped around a wooden block may be used on a flat surface. A power polisher is also useful. It is the heat developed by friction that produces the polish.

All of these methods are tedious and time consuming. One way of speeding results is to add a little varnish and turpentine to the oil. You can brush on one or two early coats of this mixture, but you should friction-polish later application with a cloth.

Instead of varnish, you can use beeswax. Dissolve about 1 ounce of beeswax in 1 pint of raw linseed oil. Heat this mixture, but do not place the linseed oil container on a hot plate or over a flame. Stand it in hot water and stir in the beeswax. Add about an equal amount of turpentine and allow the mixture to cool. Use it in the same way as the varnish-oil mixture.

There are several other mixtures, and it is possible to buy prepared oil polishes.

WAX POLISHING

Another finishing material with a long history is wax. Wax polish lasts longer than oil polish. Many modern polishes used for reviving the appearance of furniture contain wax. Prepared wax polishes are available in paste or liquid form, and some of the liquid polishes come in spray containers. Liquid wax polishes also might include cleaning agents, which remove dirt as the polish is applied. Wax finishes might be marked by heat or water.

There are many kinds of waxes, but the most popular is beeswax. Beeswax is usually white or yellowish brown.

The hardest of natural waxes is carnauba, which comes from a Brazilian palm tree. It is a pale yellow. Although brittle when used alone, it can be mixed with other waxes, and is found in many prepared wax polishes.

Paraffin wax is well known. It comes from petroleum and is a translucent white. It is soft, but can be used with other waxes. Ceresine is a hydrocarbon wax often mixed with carnauba wax.

You can buy waxes in lump or block form for making your own polish. There are also several prepared versions that come ready to use. Mixing waxes involves the use of heat, but never heat a container of wax directly on a hot plate or flame. The wax might be damaged by too much heat, and there could be risk of fire with most of them. Instead, stand the wax container in hot water, which you can keep hot by standing it over a hot plate or flame. To speed up melting shred the wax with a knife.

Turpentine is used with most waxes, either to make a liquid polish or to make a paste. A typical beeswax polish is made by melting 1 pound of shredded beeswax, then adding 1/2 pint of warmed turpentine. Stir well, then allow to cool. You can dissolve the shredded wax directly in cold turpentine, but this process takes as much as a day.

Although you can dissolve carnauba in turpentine, the resulting polish is too hard and brittle, so you must introduce another wax, such as ceresine or paraffin wax. A suitable mixture is produced by melting together 1 pound of carnauba and the other wax, and adding 1 pint of turpentine. When cooled, this will be a paste. If it is too hard, you can heat it again and add more turpentine.

Normally wax polishes are used in their natural color. The creamy or yellowish tone does not affect the appearance of the natural or stained wood underneath. If color is desired mix oil stains in while the wax is liquid. Only a small amount will be needed. You can use powdered stains, particularly if you need a brown for wax used on old furniture. An excess of coloring matter, however, might affect the polishing qualities of the wax.

You can use wax on bare wood, but the building up of a good patina is a lengthy process. Unlike oil, wax does produce a film on the surface, where oil is mostly in the wood. Consequently, there is more of the base polishing material built up to take a friction polish.

Because wax makes its own surface film and does not depend as much on penetrating the wood, it is standard procedure to seal the wood with something else before wax polishing. Wax can follow almost any of the other finishing materials, so new work can be given enough shellac, lacquer, or varnish to seal the pores before wax polishing.

If you prepare new work for wax polishing by sealing with another finish, level that finish and remove any shine before polishing. To do so, sand with finishing paper or rub down with either cloth and water or oil and pumice powder. Remove all trace of abrasive before using wax.

Although it is necessary to apply wax all over the surface, care is needed to avoid getting thick patches of wax. One way of getting an even first coat is to use a pad, very much like the one used for French polishing. Put some paste wax on a cloth then wrap it in several layers of muslin.

Cover the surface with wax, then leave it for 10 minutes or so. Rub it briskly with another cloth, first polishing in all directions, then *along* the grain. For the first polish with a hard wax, considerable friction is needed. It might help to use a brush or cloth around a brick. Initial polishing is best done by hand, but later work can be done with power tools.

After you put on the initial coat of wax polish, you can use a softer cloth for subsequent coats. Be sure to use a cloth without lint, however.

If you need to cover a large area, it might be better to concentrate on one part at a time. The final even sheen all over should not be difficult to obtain this way, especially if you do a final friction polish on the whole area.

Wax may be used to revive some other finish. Paste wax polish is the best treatment for a part that is well worn or is subject to much use. This will build up the best protective layer. However, some liquid and cream polishes will remove dirt, sticky finger marks, and similar things at the same time they polish.

Many modern wax finishes have been formulated so that little rubbing is needed and the considerable hard work of friction polishing is no longer necessary. Some of these polishes will also disguise marks left from hot or wet containers.

Some furniture polishes, intended for reviving a finish, are described as *no-rub*. Their solvent evaporates and the deposit left might have a satisfactory gloss, but a light rub will usually improve it.

Wax polishes have a reasonable shelf life. If polish becomes hard, you can melt it by placing the container in warm water and mixing in a very small amount of turpentine.

9

Special Wood Finishes

I N MODERN FURNITURE MAKING, there have been moves to introduce special effects that give wood a contemporary look. Whether these special effects are acceptable or not depends on the eye of the beholder. Many of them, however, when used with discretion, can produce striking results.

LIMING

A novel effect can be obtained on oak, chestnut, and other open-grained wood by filling the crevices of the grain with something that contrasts with the color of the wood. This process is called *liming*. The name comes from the early use of lime to whiten parts of the grain in oak. Today, other substances are used instead, such as white filler and paints.

Usually liming is done on an unstained surface—one that has been properly prepared by a final sanding with fine abrasive paper. For the best results, any bent fibers are straightened by wetting the surface and allowing it to dry before sanding.

First seal the surface with a light coat of thinned bleached shellac (2-pound cut). Several white fillers are available; some are sold specially for the purpose. You also can use a wax filler (zinc white in paraffin wax), or flat white or undercoat paint, thinned to a cream. The paint should not be too fluid or the intensity of the white might not be good enough. Apply the paint with a brush, working in all directions to force the mixture into the grain. Wipe off with a cloth to remove paint from the surface without leaving smears. If you are not satisfied the first time, you can repeat the process.

Do not sand. Sanding would deposit particles of dust and grit in the filler or paint. Allow the "lime" ample time to dry. Pine will need at least a day to dry. Cover the "lime" with another coat of the thinned, bleached shellac. Lightly sand and apply another coat of shellac. Sand again. The sanded shellac will seal the "lime" in the wood. Further treatment can be more shellac, possibly applied as French polish, or sprayed lacquer. Whatever is used should be clear, without any orange or yellow tinge.

For a variation on this process, you can stain the wood to give more contrast to the white "lime." You can obtain special effects by using stains other than brown. You can use a silver-gray water stain. A thinned black stain has a similar effect. Stains are used before any sealing. Color the wood after sanding and before applying thinned shellac sealer. Then use the chosen "lime," as already described.

Although liming is particularly appropriate to oak, you can use it on other woods with grain sufficiently open to hold the liming material. Some mahoganies will take the finish. On pine, you can use a tinted filler. You can stain pine and other softer woods gray and add a white wax filler to give a driftwood effect.

SHADING

Wood does not need to be the same shade all over, although this may seem more natural and is usual for most furniture. In some cases, there can be lighter and darker versions of the same color. On turned work, a bulbous part can be shaded lighter than the rest of the turning. In carved work, shading of the stain can increase emphasis where needed.

When shading, it is usually best to follow the color gradations of natural wear. That is, shade so that the color variations appear to be a result of aging and normal use. This is especially good advice for restoring of antiques.

There are several ways of shading. You can use a regular stain, and apply more where a darker color is wanted. If you use a spray, there can be good control. Otherwise, use a cloth as well as a brush, and let there be a gradual change from dark to light.

You can apply the stain heavily all over the surface and allow it to dry, then sand the parts that are to be lighter until the desired effect is produced.

For oil stain, apply the stain then wipe the highlighted parts with a cloth before the stain has dried.

It is also possible to apply shading after a finishing coat, particularly when spraying. There can be a first staining of the wood to what will be the lightest shading stain. After this has dried, spray more finish over it.

Plan your shading. Examine professionally made shaded furniture. Although a haphazard shading is not wanted, do not go to the other extreme and shade with geometrical precision. Follow the lines of the furniture and make the color variations gradual. At a corner, do not let the shading look like a mitered frame, but widen and round there (FIG. 9-1).

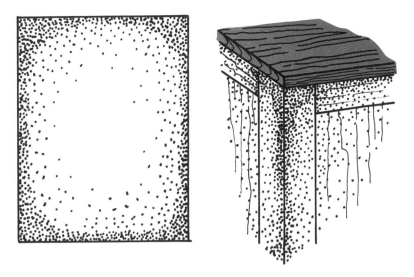

Fig. 9-1. The color graduations in shading should be gradual, especially around corners.

Shading has uses when woods are mixed in one piece of furniture. Maybe the only plywood available is not the same wood as the framing around it. Getting an exact color match by staining might be difficult. Shading, with its deliberate changing of hue, disguises the fact that the base woods are actually different.

BLOND FINISHES

Most furniture described as blond has been lightened by bleaching. Apply bleach evenly and allow it to work. Even application is important to get a uniform result. Do not use stains. The very light finish will show any defects in the wood, so choose flawless wood and take care in the workmanship.

A bleached surface left too long untreated might attract dirt or begin to become discolored. So seal it quickly, either with bleached shellac or water-white lacquer. Do not use anything that will produce a yellow tinge. Sand the sealer and follow with further finishing coats. Wax polish makes a good final treatment.

If the wood being given a blond finish is open grained, use a neutral-colored filler after bleaching and before sealing.

ACID TREATMENTS

Although stains have taken the place of many of the earlier more drastic treatments, their effect is only on the color of the wood. Some earlier treatments did things to the character of the wood, as well.

Sulfuric and nitric acid, diluted with water, will eat away the soft parts of wood and leave the harder parts standing. One part acid to three parts water is about right.

WARNING

Never pour water into acid—always acid into water. Wear a heavy rubber apron or protective clothing and heavy rubber gloves.

In softwoods, there are alternate light and dark grain lines. If acid eats away the light parts, the wood will look worn and aged. Use a wire scratch brush on the wood as you apply the acid. Wash off the acid with plenty of water and neutralize the wood with diluted ammonia before finishing. A gray stain can emphasize the apparent age, and you can follow it with wax polish.

10

Special Opaque Finishes

WHEN FURNITURE IS PAINTED with a brush or sprayed with an opaque lacquer, the colors are normally uniformly applied, even if more than one color is used. There, however, are several other ways of using opaque substances, and some of the techniques can produce very attractive results.

GRAINING

For many years, woodworkers tried to simulate the grain of wood by using paint. This technique is called graining. Graining is not an attempt to fool anyone; it is a novel way of giving wood a grainlike appearance.

You will need to use two colors: a base yellowish brown (a straw color) and a darker brown, something like the dark grain lines in spruce or fir. Apply the flat base color and allow it to dry. Then apply the second color, which is better if also flat. Allow it to partially dry. The time it is left to dry depends on the paint. Then draw a comb over the surface to scrape lines that expose the lighter color underneath. A painter's comb has broad flat teeth, but you can use a coarse hair comb. If you draw the comb along the surface with a wavy motion, the result simulates a meandering wood grain. It is possible to simulate knots by leaving circles of dark paint. When the paint dries, seal it by one or more coats of varnish or clear lacquer.

TEXTURED AND MOTTLED FINISHES

Texturing paint is a technique comparable to graining, but the result is a paint surface almost like rough plaster. There are special prepared plasters to mix with water to give this effect, but paint can be adapted. The texture treatment suits some picture frames, but is not as appropriate for larger pieces of furniture.

Give the wood one or more coats of shellac or undercoat paint to provide a base. Use a flat paint and mix into it some plaster of paris to make a thick stiff paste that can be applied with a stiff bristle brush. Put on a thick coat. Go over this surface with a stiff brush or a hair comb, either in wavy lines along the wood or in a pattern of swirls or other shapes, as desired. This will leave a pattern of ridges and hollows. Leave the work to harden.

There will usually be more roughness than is wanted, so go over the surface with medium abrasive paper to remove the high spots. Brush off any dust and give the surface a coat of paint in any shade. A gloss finish in a bright color will emphasize the texture of the surface.

To obtain a mottled effect apply one color on top of another. The lower color should be the lighter one. Apply the first and let it dry. Put the second color on. While the top color is still wet, go over it with a wad of paper, picking up some of the top paint. This process will leave a random pattern where the lighter color shows through. Let this dry, then give it a coat of clear lacquer or varnish.

Another mottled finish, suitable for frames and other narrow items, also uses two colors or dark and light versions of the same color. Apply the lighter coat and allow it to dry. Then apply the second coat with a brush or by dabbing with a cloth. Stipple with a clean cloth so some of the first coat shows through. The final effect is something like parchment. Cover with clear lacquer, varnish, or shellac.

UNEVEN EFFECTS

There are several finishes that produce an uneven finished surface. Most of them have been produced as a result of lacquer developments.

If a quick-drying lacquer is sprayed over a slow-drying elastic one, the top coat will crack. That is the principle. Spray on the first coat, using several coats if necessary. Spray the special crackle lacquer over this. In quite a short time it will crack and open up in an irregular pattern, showing the undercoat. Allow the crackle coat to dry, then cover it with a clear lacquer. With the large variety of colors available, many interesting combinations are possible. Dark blue over light blue has a clean, bright effect.

Try this technique on a practice piece first. There are no second chances with this technique.

There are special wrinkle lacquers that can be obtained in types which give different degrees of wrinkle. They can be brushed on in the usual thick consistency or thinned and sprayed. One type needs a special oven to finish it, but there is an air-dry type, although it really needs heat to form satisfactory wrinkles. Having an electric heater in the vicinity is enough. Follow the manufacturer's directions.

This is a one-coat finish, but you can change the color by spraying with ordinary lacquer. You can also obtain an interesting effect by spraying on another color with the gun angled so the new color is on only one side of the wrinkles.

Spattering is another interesting technique. Put on a base color and let it dry. Flick a second color onto the surface with a paintbrush. One way is to strike a charged paintbrush with a piece of wood, forcing flecks of paint onto the surface. Obviously, some practice on scrap wood or paper is best to master the correct technique and get the desired pattern of flecks.

The size and spacing of the flecks will depend on the distance, the amount of paint in the brush, and your handling of it. If the first spattering is too scattered for your liking, spatter more over the same area. Of course, there can be spots of different colors superimposed on each other, but allow each color to dry before you apply the next.

MARBLING

Another skill of old-time painters was the production of a surface that looked like marble. The painter got this effect by using a fine brush or a feather. You can use this method to create an interesting finish on just about any flat wood surface.

Apply a light flat paint to the surface. Usually two colors are used for marbling, in addition to the initial flat coat. Blue and red are suitable, but marble has many hues, mostly in mild pastel shades. Dip the end of a feather in one color and pull the feather across the painted surface, moving it about in a wavy random pattern, varying the pressure so as to get different widths and intensities of line. Do the same thing with the second color. Where the wet colors join, they will blend into each other as they do at some points in marble. Get a meandering mixed pattern of lines and curves that have some thin, hairlike parts and some quite thick areas.

Allow the marbled surface to fully dry. Then cover it with a waterproof or heatproof lacquer.

11

Decorating

THERE ARE SEVERAL WAYS of altering the appearance of wood surfaces without actually applying a finish. These techniques come under the heading of decorating.

STENCILS

Many pieces of furniture, both modern and period, can be improved considerably by stenciling designs on them in contrasting colors. Ready-made stencils are available at paint and art supply stores, but it is easy to make your own. Simply draw or trace out the design you want, then cut it out with a very sharp knife or a razor blade. The cuts must be neat or the final transfer will have rough edges. After the stencil has been cut out, coat it with shellac or lacquer to stiffen the paper. Then place the stencil on the work and hold it securely with masking tape. Make sure you mask sufficiently if you are using a spray can or sprayer.

You can apply paint either with a spray can, a spray gun, or a stencil brush. Painting with a spray unit will produce better results than applying the paint by hand, but make sure that the paint doesn't spread too thick or too thin. Also make sure the paint doesn't get under the masking tape. If you plan to brush the paint on, use a special stencil brush, available at larger hardware and building material retailers. Art shops have them, too.

Ordinary paint is too thin for good stenciling. Oil colors are superior. Make sure the paint you select indicates that it can be used for stenciling.

Once the paint is dry, remove the stencil. Then protect the design against wear with a thin coat of clear varnish.

DECALS

This history of slide-on transfer pictures goes back many years, but many of the early techniques had faults. It is now possible to get decals that work very satisfactorily, and the number of different kinds of decals seems endless.

Application methods vary, so first read the directions carefully. Most decals can be affixed to just about any flat wood surface, but any unevenness or raised grain may show through. So it is usually best to prepare a surface and apply at least one or two coats of finish before affixing decals. If the final finish is clear varnish or lacquer, the decal can go on before the last coat is applied. If the finish is paint, the decal can be applied over the top coat, but this method leaves the decal vulnerable to abrasion.

Most decals are quite tough, but it is better to give some more protection with a coat of clear varnish or lacquer. The solvents in some clear finishes might cause the decal to crack or loosen. Decals cannot be applied over wax or many other polishes, so clean these surfaces first with a solvent.

PAPERING

Wall coverings also can be applied to furniture. Papering produces special effects and can conceal irreparable flaws. Some modern decorators paper furniture panels to match surrounding walls. Such a combination can be striking. Modern plastic-coated wall coverings provide quite a durable finish, which can be cleaned when necessary without damaging the paper. Usually a contact adhesive paper should be used on furniture; conventional paste wallpaper comes away too easily.

The surface of the wood should be level. The paper can ease into cracks or holes, so smooth the surface smooth with filler. If the surface is dirty, clean with alcohol or other solvent.

Applying contact paper to furniture is a straightforward process. Peel the backing off and place one edge of the contact paper on the surface being covered. Rub this edge down and lower the rest of the paper gradually, pressing it down little by little (FIG. 11-1). It is possible to lift and reposition to a limited extent, but too much adjustment might weaken the final hold of the adhesive. You can use a roller, but stroke out wrinkles and air bubbles by hand. When you have the paper right, go over it again with plenty of pressure.

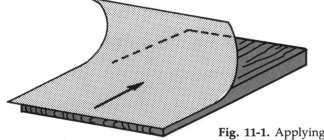

Fig. 11-1. Applying contact paper.

Trim edges with a razor blade or a sharp knife. The paper will wrap over angles. To cover an edge (like a table edge), cut the paper as shown in FIG. 11-2. Fold one flap down and around the corner. Fold the other flap down and smooth it out (FIG. 11- 3).

Fig. 11-2. Covering edges with contact paper.

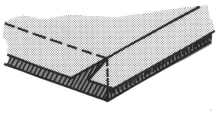

Fig. 11-3. In covering an edge with contact paper, the flaps should be overlapped precisely.

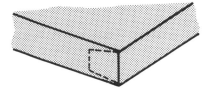

MOLDINGS AND CARVINGS

Suppliers of materials for furniture making prepare shallow carvings and lengths of molding that can be applied to flat surfaces. The cheapest carvings are embossed. They have their patterns pressed on. There are also comparable plastic simulated carvings.

Moldings may be simple beads (FIG. 11-4) or carved patterns (FIG. 11-5). Carvings may be simple button motifs or elaborate floral clusters (FIG. 11-6).

Fig. 11-4. Some moldings are beads.

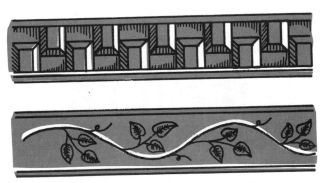

Fig. 11-5. Moldings can be carved patterns of all kinds.

Fig. 11-6. Carvings for wood decorations, such as this floral design, can be very intricate.

You can use moldings or strip carvings to give interest to an otherwise plain flat surface (FIG. 11-7). Use other carvings to provide a center of interest, as on a pelmet over drapes (FIG. 11-8). You can glue these applied decorations in place, but it's a good idea to reinforce the glue with a few tiny nails.

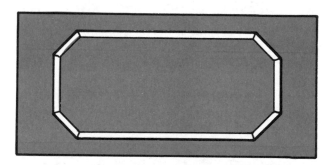

Fig. 11-7. Strips of molding can be used to add interest to plain surfaces.

Fig. 11-8. Carvings can provide a focal point for furniture.

PYROGRAPHY

Pyrography is a modern name for what was once called pokerwork, from its original form in which a hot poker was used to burn patterns into wood. The modern alternative to the poker is electrically heated and is something like a small electric soldering iron.

Hold the tool like a pen and use it to draw patterns of burnt lines on the wood. You can vary the widths of lines with different points or by tilting a universal head. The speed of working also affects the intensity of line and its depth.

Use pyrograph with restraint on most furniture; however, it will add interest to children's furniture and a few kitchen items.

You can use pyrography in combination with color for decoration in places where a decal might otherwise be used. Outline the pattern by burning and color the spaces. The result looks something like a stained glass window.

Pyrograph is burning, so the wood is charred and some ash is produced. For a clean result, lightly brush or blow away these particles, then give the surface a coat or two of clear varnish or lacquer to prevent further spreading of any burnt dust.

FLOCK SPRAYING

There are methods that can give a wood surface a clothlike appearance, not by putting on pieces of cloth, but by spraying particles of flock over an adhesive. Flock usually consists of short or pulverized fiber. Usually, the result of these techniques looks like felt. Flock usually is applied by spraying. Many colors are available.

It is possible to spray almost anything. A complete piece of furniture can be covered. A drawer can be lined with flock for jewelry or cutlery.

The important tool is a hand-operated spray gun, which has a turbulation chamber to swirl the fibers as they are ejected. Usually, flock is sprayed onto a sticky undercoat that is the same color as the flock.

Section II
REPAIRING
FURNITURE

12

Dealing With Minor Damage

IN ADDITION TO FINISH DAMAGE, a piece of furniture might suffer damage that affects it structurally. Of course, structural damage might warrant the replacement of a part or the splicing on of a major new section, but there are many ways to fix existing weakened or broken parts. Usually this means less work than replacing parts. In many cases, preserving the original material can be extremely important.

REGLUING

A common fault is the breaking down of a glued joint without the wood becoming fractured. There are two versions of this problem: joints that are loose but cannot be pulled apart because other parts of the structure are holding them, and joints that can be taken apart.

The repaired joint will be stronger if you can remove most of the old glue because some glues are not compatible with others. If you cannot scrape the old glue away because it is inaccessible, you should supplement the joint with screws, nails, or dowels.

If you can separate a joint, use a scraper or a chisel to remove chunks of glue. Then scratch the joint surfaces with an awl or a saw to break through to expose new surfaces (FIG. 12-1). Inside a mortise, or hole, use the awl to scratch through the old glue. The important thing is to tear into the surfaces so fibers untainted by the old glue are exposed without reducing the surface as a whole.

If the parts of the joint have become very open as a result of rocking, it is inadvisable to depend solely on glue to fill the spaces. It might be possible

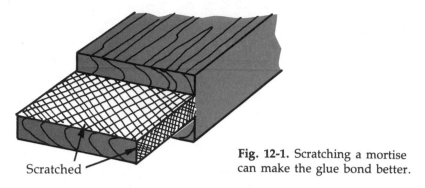

Scratched

Fig. 12-1. Scratching a mortise can make the glue bond better.

to insert a wood shaving alongside a tenon to build up the surface (with glue all around it of course). You could wrap a shaving, or even a piece of paper, around a loose dowel. If all else fails, mix sawdust with the glue so it becomes a puttylike paste. Use the mixture in the joint. Be careful not to starve the joint of glue in some places. It might be better to use the more fluid, ordinary glue deeper in the hole and put the sawdust/glue only where needed.

If you cannot separate a joint fully, it will almost certainly wobble enough to expose part of the inside. All surfaces you can reach should be freed of old glue as far as possible and scratched to penetrate the fibers. Much can be done with a slim knife blade and fine awl. A razor blade will sometimes be useful. If there is an open part within a joint that you cannot reach, squirt liquid glue in with a syringe.

Fig. 12-2. A glue/sawdust mixture can be pressed into a joint with a knife.

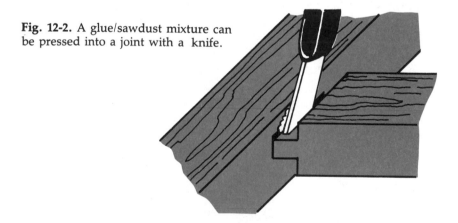

It might also be possible to use the glue/sawdust mixture a little at a time and press it progressively into the hidden part of the joint with a knife (FIG. 12-2). Such a joint might finish with adequate strength from the glue only, but it is unlikely that new glue will penetrate sufficiently, particularly if it is a joint that does not open very far. Consequently, further strengthening might be advisable. You should strengthen it before the glue has hardened and before any clamps are removed. Use clamps with blocks to spread the pressure and reduce the risk of marking surfaces. You also can place cloth or paper between a block and a surface for further protection. Round the edges of blocks used as pads to avoid an abrupt change which could mark a finished surface (FIG. 12-3).

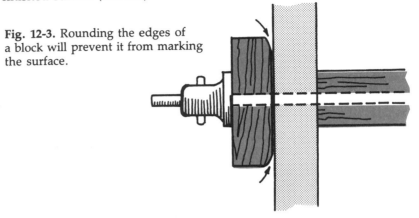

Fig. 12-3. Rounding the edges of a block will prevent it from marking the surface.

Watch a joint as pressure is applied. See that it is going together straight. Don't squeeze excessively. Stop when the joint is obviously closed. Putting on more pressure after that will only distort fibers, either at the joint, or worse, on the surfaces under the pressure pads. Leave clamps in position until you are certain the glue has set.

REINFORCING JOINTS

A simple reinforcement is to use nails, preferably driven from a less obvious surface, like the inside of a table leg (FIG. 12-4). As with clamping, take the precaution of supporting the opposite surface on a padded solid support to minimize any risk of damage to the finish.

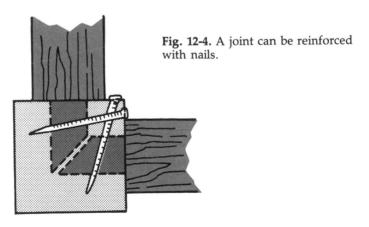

Fig. 12-4. A joint can be reinforced with nails.

If, however, you have a choice, use screws for joint reinforcement. If there is a clearance hole for the neck of the screw and a hole to aid penetration through the dowel or tenon (FIG. 12-5), some expansion will take place as the screw is driven. The expansion will strengthen the joint by pushing the glued surfaces closer together. Remember that the glue still must be soft.

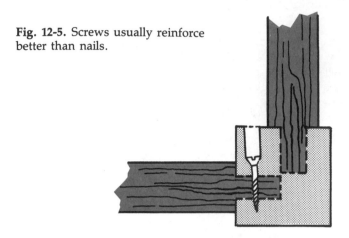

Fig. 12-5. Screws usually reinforce better than nails.

For larger joints, better reinforcement comes from the use of dowels instead of nails or screws. Dowels should not be so large as to weaken the inner wood by drilling away too much, but a diameter of dowel about the same as the thickness of a tenon or not more than half the thickness of the constructional dowel would be satisfactory. Drill into the clamped joint enough to allow the dowel to go through the mating parts without breaking out the opposite side (FIG. 12-6).

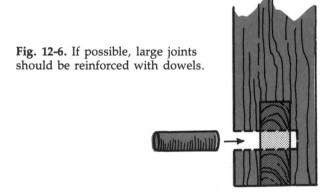

Fig. 12-6. If possible, large joints should be reinforced with dowels.

If the joint can be taken apart, you can make an even more secure dowel-reinforced joint. Drill the center for the hole in the inner part independently, slightly nearer where the parts abut, so when the joint is assembled the holes do not quite match (FIG. 12-7). Bevel the end of the dowel so it will enter the offset hole as it is driven and pull the parts closer together as it forces its way through.

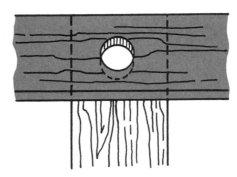

Fig. 12-7. Holes drilled separately will not exactly match. When the dowel is inserted, the disparity will help to pull the parts of the joint together.

If a tenon has broken off or is so damaged that there would be insufficient strength if it was reglued, you can make a new tenon by scarfing it into a long groove (FIG. 12-8). Making the groove twice as long as it is deep should give adequate gluing surface.

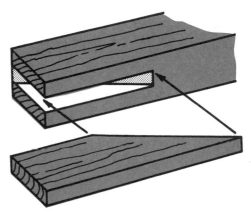

Fig. 12-8. Some reinforcements call for tenons to be scarfed into long grooves.

When a dowel breaks off, it is usually possible to drill into the broken piece to remove it so a new dowel can be glued in. To reduce the risk of the drill straying or starting off-center, level the broken end and mark the center with a deep dot from a center punch or awl (FIG. 12-9). If the mating hole is worn out of shape, it might be better to use a slightly larger diameter new dowel and open out the worn hole to the new size with a suitable drill. Be careful not to weaken either of the parts by drilling away too much wood. If the larger size would shave surrounding wood dangerously thin, you might want to keep to the same size and rely on filling spaces with glue and sawdust or shavings. If there is sufficient wood to allow dowels to penetrate farther, you can gain strength by drilling deeper.

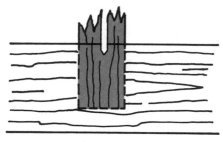

Fig. 12-9. If you are drilling out an old dowel, first mark its center with a punch.

A dowel entering a hole acts something like a piston in a cylinder, compressing the air inside, with the risk of bursting the hole, often pushing glue aside or into the bottom of the hole so the more important surfaces around the circumference of the dowel are left with little or no glue. When fitting a new dowel, bevel the ends and make a groove in the length (FIG. 12-10) with a saw or any tool that will scratch a slight hollow. The dowel will drive in without catching, and any excess glue and the compressed air will find its way out through the groove, resulting in a tight joint with a good spread of glue.

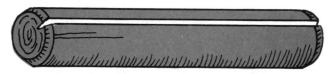

Fig. 12-10. Before inserting a new dowel, bevel its edge and groove the side.

If the joint is so weakened that repairs within the structure might not be adequate, use further reinforcement. In most such structures, the inside is not normally viewed, so strengthening can be done there. If there is room, glue in wood blocks or fasten with thin nails driven diagonally (FIG. 12-11).

Fig. 12-11. A corner of a structure can sometimes be reinforced with a block.

If there has been any surface treatment, scrape it away and roughen the exposed wood before gluing. Even if there has not been any surface treatment, give the surfaces a light scraping to remove dirt and present a new surface to the joint. It might be possible to merely rub the blocks in the glue and leave them without clamping, if the design is such that there is no way of using clamps.

In a corner where two rails join a leg, it might be better to make a wooden bracket fitted around the parts (FIG. 12-12). This bracket could be fixed with glue, but the end grain, because of the diagonal cut, might not give the best gripping surface for glue. You can strengthen the joint and pull it tight by screws driven at an angle (FIG. 12-13). If you cut the bracket with slightly too wide an angle, its points will meet the rails first; further tightening closes the entire joint.

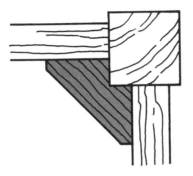

Fig. 12-12. A wooden bracket can be used to strengthen a corner.

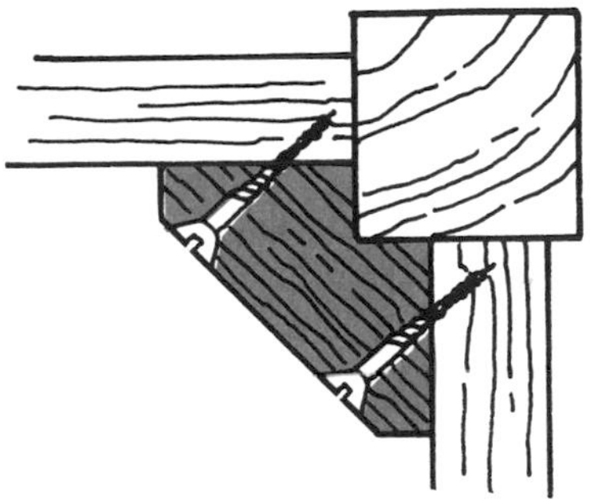

Fig. 12-13. A wooden bracket in a corner can be fastened down with screws.

Fig. 12-14. Strips of wood can be used to reinforce angles of all kinds.

You can use similar wood blocks in other joints. A tabletop can have blocks or a continuous strip fastened to the supporting rail (FIG. 12-14). There are plastic and metal strips intended for use in angles of ready-to-assemble furniture or adjustable shelves. Some are blocks to be screwed in both directions, like the wood blocks, and others are in two parts with a machine screw to pull them together (FIG. 12-15). The two-part type is useful in a repair where one structure tends to pull away from another because of warping, twisting, or other cause.

Fig. 12-15. Parts can be pulled together with blocks and screws.

Another way of dealing with a loose top on surrounding rails is to use pocket screwing. Drill a hole diagonally from inside, and cut out a notch to let the screw head pull in (FIG. 12-16). For the greatest strength, the point of the screw needs to go as far as possible into the top, so take care to drill adequately without actually breaking through the top.

Metal repair plates are available in flat, straight, and angled patterns of various sizes. In furniture where they can be hidden, they can provide rigidity in a repair, often greater than is possible by any wood reinforcing. You can fasten an angle plate into the underside of a weak miter joint or behind the corner of a picture or mirror frame (FIG. 12-17).

You can use a straight repair plate where two adjoining parts must be held together. You can use the angle type of bracket inside corners, as in an old chest where the sides no longer hold together. There is not much that can be done to make a bracket draw a joint tight, but there are a couple of tricks that might help. If you spring an angled bracket so it is slightly less than at right angle, it will have a slight tightening effect as it is screwed down. It is also helpful to drill for screws toward the corner (FIG. 12-18). As the screw head pulls down into the countersink of the bracket, it will pull the corner tighter.

Another device with some repair applications is the corrugated fastener. The corrugations are at a slight angle on each side of the center, so as it is driven, a joint across its center is pulled closer. The device might be considered crude and mostly only suitable for rough carpentry, but in a place like the underside of a plinth, it is a good reinforcement (FIG. 12-19). Another method for corner joining is to cut the head off a nail and file a second point, then bend the ends and drive them in hard enough to bury the whole nail flush with the surface (FIG. 12-20).

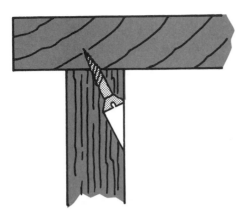

Fig. 12-16. Pocket screwing is another way to pull parts together.

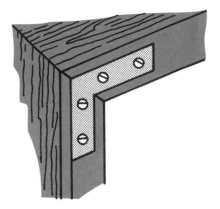

Fig. 12-17. Miter joints can be secured with angle plates.

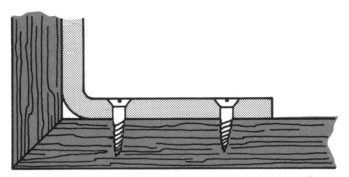

Fig. 12-18. Angle plates should be fastened on with screws near the corner.

Fig. 12-19 Corrugated fasteners can be used to pull a miter joint together.

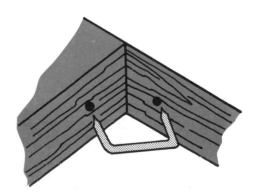

Fig. 12-20. Double-pointed nails can be used to reinforce a miter joint.

REESTABLISHING SCREWS

Sometimes screws no longer hold in the wood. This problem might occur at the hinges of a heavy door or at a frequently used fitting. The simple answer is a larger screw, but this solution might not be practicable, particularly when the hole in a metal fitting is involved. There might be no room for a larger screw head, particularly in a hinge, and the result might look clumsy on some fittings. A longer screw of the same diameter might gain extra hold at the point, but point hold might last for only a short time.

Most stoppings and wood plastics do not have much strength, so it would not be satisfactory to plug a hole with them and drive the screw again. You might be able to push a sliver of wood into the hole and drive the screw again, but this method tends to push the screw out of line. Most glues crystalize and break away after setting around a screw, so they would not provide strength. The only adhesive that would secure a slackened screw would be epoxy glue. It will bond to both the metal and the wood. It will adhere so strongly that it might be impossible to withdraw the screw later.

An alternative, particularly where large screws are involved, is to drill out the hole and insert a plug. The plug can be a piece of dowel rod (FIG. 12-21). Take it slightly deeper than the screw is to penetrate, glue it in place, and drill again as if starting a new screw. Make a clearance hole for the screw neck and an undersize hole for the threaded part.

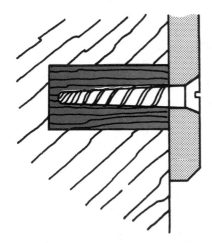

Fig. 12-21. Sometimes a plug is the best way to hold a screw in place.

Instead of a piece of dowel rod, you can use one of the plugs intended for fixing to masonry, either a fibrous or a plastic type. Plastic plugs are especially useful in particleboard (FIG. 12-22).

Screws do not hold well in end grain. Even if you make a repair by plugging the hole, there might be a risk of the joint coming away. Another way of using a dowel to reinforce a screw driven with the grain is to arrange it across the wood at a position where the screw can go into it (FIG. 12-23).

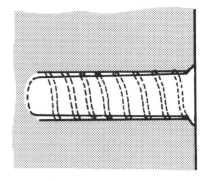

Fig. 12-22. A plastic plug inserted in particleboard.

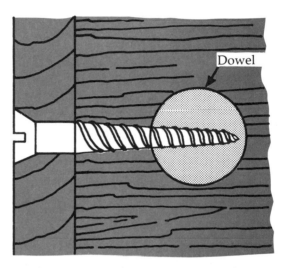

Dowel

Fig. 12-23. A screw inserted in a dowel will hold better than a screw forced into regular wood.

The dowel need not go right through. You can drill the hole from a hidden surface without breaking through any exposed surface. Position the dowel so the screw can have as many threads as possible in the cross grain of the dowel.

ADDING NEW WOOD

When new wood must be added to furniture in order to make repairs, one of the first considerations is matching the grain. Ideally, the repair will be made with wood of the same kind. Although a careful craftsman might make the new part exactly to size and achieve a perfect match, it would be much easier to join on an oversize piece of wood and bring the new wood to size after it has become an extension of the old part. Even with the greatest care, it is possible to find a slight error of alignment or of matching shape after joining on, so leaving a little surplus wood permits adjustment.

An example is a fractured edge. Say the damage is cut away at an angle, both in the length and across the edge (FIG. 12-24). You can cut a new piece approximately to shape and glue it on (FIG. 12-25), then plane off the surplus wood. This is a simple example, but you can use this same technique with a part that must be worked to a curve or carved after fixing. Match the grain, leave enough spare wood to work on, then treat the part as a whole when the glue has set. In this way, the new work will blend into the old.

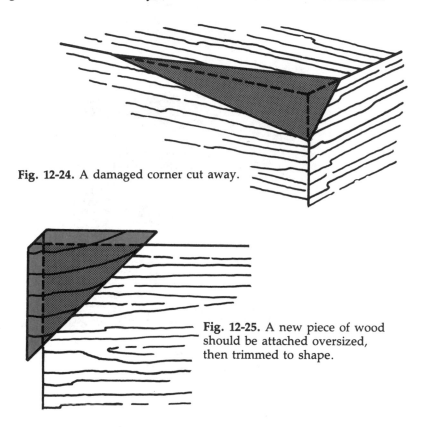

Fig. 12-24. A damaged corner cut away.

Fig. 12-25. A new piece of wood should be attached oversized, then trimmed to shape.

If it is necessary to join on a complete new piece, you can have a lapped joint or a splice. The new part usually can be identical to the old, but if the old part is curved, the new piece should have extra wood for working into shape (FIG. 12-26).

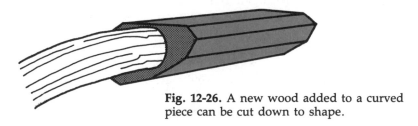

Fig. 12-26. A new wood added to a curved piece can be cut down to shape.

If the edge of a long piece (like a square table leg) must be cut away for repairs, cut away the ends of the replacement part at angles (FIG. 12-27). This cut makes for a much better fit. If you make the cuts carefully, you can form a very inconspicuous joint. The action of clamping the open end will force the other end tightly into the acute angle. If you can get to the repair easily after gluing, it is helpful to leave considerable excess wood to be cleaned off later. Tool marks can be cut away during finishing to size. In a less accessible place, it might be better to cut the repair piece close to size.

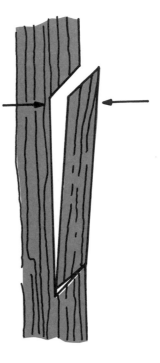

Fig. 12-27. A replacement piece for an edge should be cut at an angle.

Sometimes new wood must be inset into a damaged surface. First look at the piece from several angles before cutting out. A simple rectangle puts two cuts *across* the grain. Even with careful fitting, these cuts are likely to remain apparent (FIG. 12-28). An ellipse with its long axis in the direction of the grain will be less obvious (FIG. 12-29), but having a curve brings problems in cutting and fitting. Another alternative is to use a long diamond shape (FIG. 12-30). This shape avoids cuts directly across the grain so it is easier to disguise.

If the damage is within reasonable distance from an end, it might be better to make the replacement part continue out to the end. This procedure will reduce the number of cuts not directly along the grain (FIG. 12-31). A further step, if the surface is not too big, is to extend the replacement part out to both ends. Then the only joints will be *with* the grain and might pass as normal joints between boards making up the top.

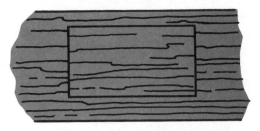

Fig. 12-28. Inlaid wood is sometimes quite conspicuous.

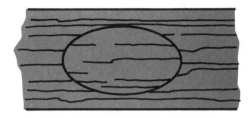

Fig. 12-29. A ellipse-shaped piece usually makes a less conspicuous inlay.

Fig. 12-30. A long diamond-shaped inlay.

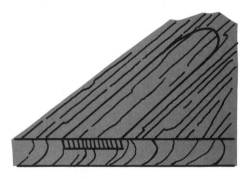

Fig. 12-31. A replacement part that is inlaid from the edge inward.

For a surface repair, there is no need to cut more deeply than necessary to remove the damage. You can chop out the wood or remove it with a router. A power router ensures an even depth cleanly cut, but the unevenness from cutting out with a chisel will not matter. No matter how deep the damage is, it is advisable with most woods to go at least 1/4 inch deep. A thin replacement piece might warp eventually. Trim the edges of the routed area vertically, but make the repair piece with slightly beveled edges (FIG. 12-32).

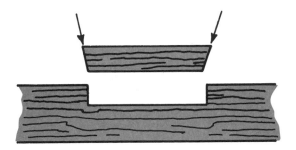

Fig. 12-32. A repair inlay should have beveled edges.

It is best to proceed slowly. Cut the recess approximately to shape and make the replacement patch slightly larger than the first recess cuts. Trim the patch to its final shape. Use it with the underside downward as a template to mark the final shape of the recess, preferably marking with a sharp thin-bladed knife. Trim the recess to shape and try the patch in place, but do not press it in.

The patch should be slightly too thick. Glue it in place and press it down with paper under a wood block (FIG. 12-33). Use clamps if possible. Failing that, hand pressure might get the patch in, then you can place weights on top until the glue has set. Finally, plane and sand the patch level.

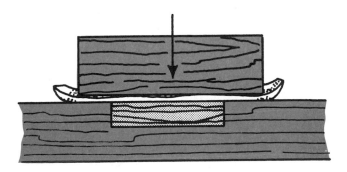

Fig. 12-33. Press the inlay down with a wooden block. Use paper between the block and the inlay.

Before the days of plywood, blockboard, and particleboard, the only way to make a broad panel like a tabletop was to join boards edge to edge (FIG. 12-34). Such a built-up panel can easily warp, shrink, expand, or otherwise distort. Much old furniture was built with built-up panels, however. It is not sufficient to repair such panels by fixing stout battens underneath because the wood needs to expand and contract. Even with properly seasoned wood, a tabletop 2 feet wide might expand and shrink as much as 1/4 inch in the width because of changes in temperature and humidity.

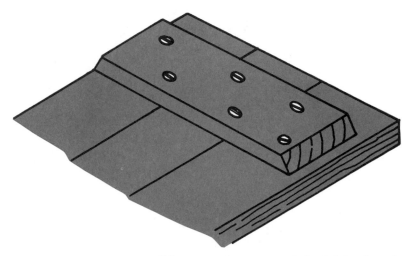

Fig. 12-34. At one time, all large panels were made by joining boards edge to edge.

Of course, if the piece of furniture is not an antique or there is no reason for keeping the old top, it might be better to replace it with a new top made from manufactured board. If you want to retain the old top, screw on any battens put across it without glue, and each screw should have a slot (except perhaps the center one). A round hole for the center screw keeps the batten central, but the slots will allow some movement (FIG. 12-35). The amount of movement to expect depends on many factors, but allowing too much is better than not enough, so 1/2-inch slots are reasonable.

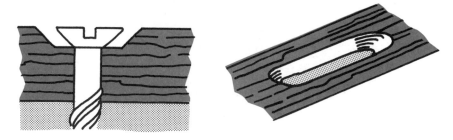

Fig. 12-35. Screw slots allow for movement.

13

Veneering

THE PROCESS OF VENEERING consists of gluing together sheets of thin wood upon a solid base. There are several reasons for veneering. A rather plain base wood can be covered by a decorative veneer. Expensive solid wood can be avoided by using a cheap base wood veneered with a layer of the expensive wood to achieve a similar appearance to the solid wood. Some woods, particularly those with attractive grains might not be suitable for use in solid form, or they might not be available in pieces large enough for furniture.

VENEERING

Early veneers were sawn by hand, and therefore were comparatively thick by modern standards. Old furniture can be found with these thick veneers, and it is unlikely that new veneer of comparable thickness will be available. For patching, you might be able to build up the thickness with several layers of modern veneer. Sometimes, working on antique furniture means cutting your own veneers, but fortunately with a power saw instead of a hand saw.

Modern veneers can be cut by saw or knife, depending on the wood and its grain or the effect desired. Most modern veneers are cut from logs by a stationary knife. The log rotates as the knife slices off a thin layer of wood. Plywood is made up of veneers laid across each other, but these ply veneers are usually thicker than those intended to be laid on a solid backing.

Allied with wood veneers are the plastic laminates, used to provide tough working surfaces that are immune to many of the liquids which attack wood and mark many finishes. Some of these plastic laminates can be given a wood grain appearance. Some even have genuine wood veneer embedded in clear plastic. There is, however, no attempt to deceive anyone into thinking the plastic is genuine wood, although some of the plastic laminates have an appearance remarkably close to the genuine article.

You should not use plastic laminates on old furniture if the piece is to retain its authenticity. If this is unimportant, you can use plastic laminate, such as Formica, to give a new life and appearance to something like a battered tabletop that is beyond refurbishing in any other way.

There are plastic veneers available. They are not really veneers in the cabinetmaking sense, but are more like paper and can be used in covering plain furniture to give a decorative effect. These materials are supplied as unbacked sheets to be stuck down with the adhesive, or have the veneer on a paper backing, which must be soaked or peeled off. You can wrap the material over edges and trim with a razor blade or sharp knife after fixing.

Some plastic veneers have grain effects, which simulate the appearance of real wood. Don't expect too much of these thin pieces of plastic, but they do have a reasonable life span as temporary covering for utility furniture. Light-patterned plastic veneer, or even wallpaper, can be used to brighten the inside of a drawer. This is particularly suitable where age has given the wood an unattractive appearance.

A further variation is genuine veneer in strip form with paper backing. The strips are designed to cover edges. They are available to match the veneers used on manufactured boards, or with veneered boards that have bare edges. You can apply the veneer strips by hand pressure after you have stripped the backing.

If you intend to use veneer on a base wood, you should consider what stresses it will need to endure. If the base wood is fairly substantial and firmly fixed, there should be no problem, but if the base wood is light, there is a risk of distortion if veneer is applied to one side only. The distortion happens over a period of maybe a year; the veneered surface might pull hollow. You can counteract this problem by veneering both sides. If the second side is unimportant, the veneer used there can be a cheap plain one.

MATERIALS

Veneers are available in panels and natural pieces. It is unlikely that you will need a large piece in a repair, but remember that a sawn veneer cannot be any wider than the tree trunk from which it was cut, so you might need to make up widths by joining edges.

Knife-cut veneers produced on a rotary machine can be almost any width. At one time, knife-cut veneers were supplied in several thicknesses, stock veneers in the quality decorative woods are nearly all in standard thicknesses. Most veneers produced in America are 1/28 inch thick. This is slightly under 1 inch. English veneers (some of which are imported) may be 1/40 inch thick.

A lot of very old furniture has inlaid bands or borders made up of pieces of veneer arranged in patterns. These veneers range from 1/8 to 1 inch in thickness. They were laid in or around veneered panels or sometimes inset into solid wood. Although it would be possible to make up a section of banding in a repair, it would be very tedious and it might be difficult to get a sufficient variety of veneers to match the existing work. Fortunately, these bands are still available ready-made, and it is likely that one of the stock patterns will match the old work, since the designs continue traditional patterns.

Some of these borders use materials other than wood. Celluloid was used, being one of the earliest uses of synthetic plastics in furniture. Brass was also included, and imitation tortoiseshell was used to produce a glisten. Musical instruments often had these special bands.

TOOLS

You can make most minor repairs to veneer without special tools. If you understand the tools and techniques required for fixing large pieces of veneer, more ambitious repairs or complete replacements are possible.

Veneers are quite fragile and are susceptible to splitting and breaking, so handle them carefully and keep them between boards to protect them and reduce warping and twisting, which can be very marked in some woods.

Cutting can be done on a piece of stout plywood or a piece of hardboard over a solid support. Most cutting can be done with a sharp thin-bladed knife used against a straightedge or template. Cut so that any tendency for the knife to catch in the grain will be toward the waste part (FIG. 13-1), if the cut is not directly across or along the grain. If there is a risk of breaking out at the end of a cut toward an edge, cut both ways, from the ends toward the center.

Fig. 13-1. Lay the straightedge along the cutting line. Shield the pattern side with the straightedge so that a mistake will damage only the waste wood.

All ordinary saws are too coarse for cutting veneers, but there are saws with very fine teeth that you can use along a straightedge or around a template. The handle is offset to allow for this procedure (FIG. 13-2). A knife, by the nature of its action, leaves a slight bevel on an edge, but a saw can produce a vertical cut. So if no finishing work is to be done on an edge, a saw should produce a closer joint than a knife. However, edges often must be trimmed for a final fit with a chisel or finely set small block plane. These tools can correct the bevel from a knife.

There are several special tools for trimming edges after veneer has been laid. One has a knife in a handle like a plane. Another is like a chisel with a hollow end. For normal repair work, a chisel, knife, or plane will do all the trimming needed. You should purchase special tools only if you intend to do a large amount of veneering.

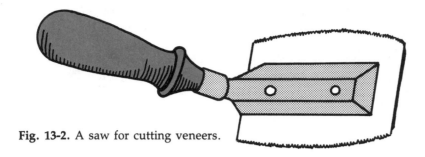

Fig. 13-2. A saw for cutting veneers.

Laying a veneer usually means roughing up the base surface so the glue can get a better grip. This can be done by pulling saw teeth sideways.

Veneers are laid on glue and must be pressed down and maintained in contact until the glue has set. You can use most of the glues already described, but there are advantages to using a water-soluble heat-sensitive glue, particularly when you are repairing old veneering fixed originally with animal or fish glue. If you cannot obtain this sort of glue, one of the white glues in squeeze bottles should be satisfactory. There is some advantage in using a quick-setting glue: the veneer becomes secure in a short time and pressure need only be brief.

Another problem might be staining. Veneers are so thin that glue might soak right through them. They might not spoil adhesion, but there might be a stain showing on the surface after the glue has dried. You usually cannot sand out the stain because the wood is permeated. The only treatment is bleaching. It is better to use a glue known not to penetrate.

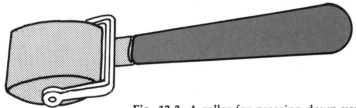

Fig. 13-3. A roller for pressing down veneers.

You can press veneers down with a roller, which might be a handled type (FIG. 13-3) or even an old pastry roller. You also can use a veneer hammer, which is similar to a squeegee (FIG. 13-4). To use this tool, place both hands on the handle or one hand over the hammer's head. Draw the hammer, using plenty of pressure, in a zigzag manner across the veneer (FIG. 13-5). The object is to bring the veneer and the base surface into the closest contact and to work any surplus glue or air bubbles to the edges. For small repairs, draw a hammer with a cross peen across the newly glued part in the same way.

If you are using a quick-setting glue, prolonged pressure is unnecessary, but in traditional gluing of veneers, large areas were clamped in a *caul*. The caul was merely an arrangement of boards (blockboard today) with strips across the clamps at the ends (FIG. 13-6). The cross strips were curved along the bottom so pressure could be maintained at the center and along the full width (FIG. 13-7). The caul is still a good tool to use today.

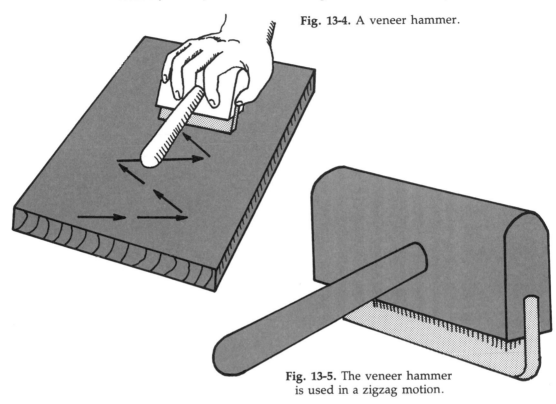

Fig. 13-4. A veneer hammer.

Fig. 13-5. The veneer hammer is used in a zigzag motion.

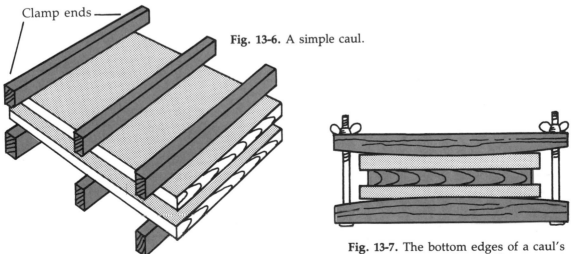

Clamp ends

Fig. 13-6. A simple caul.

Fig. 13-7. The bottom edges of a caul's cross strips are curved so uniform pressure can be maintained.

REPAIRS

A common fault in old veneer is a blister. The glue underneath has ceased to hold and a bubblelike projection has appeared. The blister might be a result of moisture soaking through or excessive heat. You can detect blisters early by tapping over the surface with the knuckle. A different note will indicate failure of the glue.

Use a razor blade or very fine knife to cut with the grain along what is judged to be the center of the blister. Do not go any further than necessary. Use the point of a knife to insert glue into the bubble (FIG. 13-8). Do this to both sides, but be careful not to break or slit the fibers of the veneer. If it is a large blister, it might be possible to get more glue in with the fingers. By surface pressure and stroking, try to spread the glue to the furthermost parts.

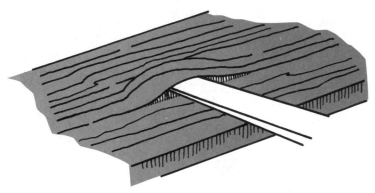

Fig. 13-8. Once a wood blister is slit, a knife can be used to insert glue.

Press down, moderately at first, working from the edges of the blister to the cut. Wipe away any surplus glue with a damp cloth. Use a roller, veneer hammer, or a cross peen hammer to finally press down. If it is necessary to apply more prolonged pressure, put paper over the blister and a block of wood over that. Use a clamp if possible or put weights on the block.

If a small area has been damaged, it is sometimes possible to disguise it with some sort of stopping, as described in Section 3. Except for the most minor damage, however, it is better to cut it away and insert a new piece. It is usually possible to cut through the veneer and pry it away.

To avoid marking the surrounding undamaged veneer, it is advisable to work in two stages. With a pencil, outline the area to be replaced and cut inside the outline to get the waste out from that area, (FIG. 13-9). Then trim to the limits of the outline. Try to scrape old glue away down to the wood, without going too deeply.

Repairing damaged veneers near an edge is usually pretty simple. Cut out a long V enclosing the damage and make a patch to go in. Let the piece stick out a bit along the edge and trim it after the glue has set (FIG. 13-10).

Fig. 13-9. Cutting inside the outlined damaged area.

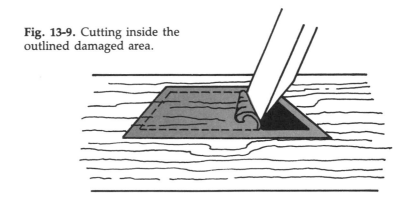

Fig. 13-10. Repairing veneer damage near an edge.

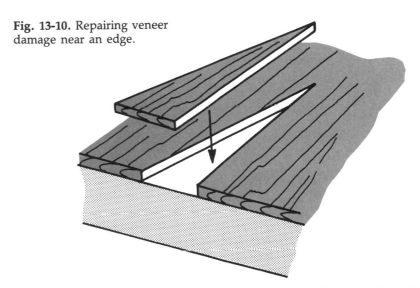

Any sort of cut will show when the repair has been finished. Usually the main problem is making the patch fit the opening. A bad fit is more obvious with irregular cuts; straight cuts usually create better fits. Irregular cuts, however, can be made with better precision with special punches. Each punch has a cutting end, which works like a leather punch, but the cutting end has an irregular shape (FIG. 13-11). The punch cuts around the defect. Then it cuts a perfectly matching patch on the new veneer that should glue in to be practically unnoticeable.

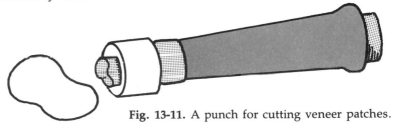

Fig. 13-11. A punch for cutting veneer patches.

A lot of veneering looks like solid wood, with a very normal looking grain. Veneers also lend themselves to patterns, however. Four panels might be arranged around a center, with a border of veneer cut across the grain (FIG. 13-12). There are many elaborations on this and other built-up patterns of varying complexity. The making of pictures in marquetry is an example. Some cabinetmakers use veneers in different woods and shapes to make patterns. A chess board is an example.

Fig. 13-12. Veneers can be laid in patterns.

When a repair involves the replacement of parts of several adjoining veneers in one of these patterned panels, it is usually best to prefabricate the built-up patch and fit it in as a unit. If you must cut two pieces of veneer to match each other, it is usually possible to cut both at once. Allow a little surplus at the meeting edges. Let them overlap and slice or saw through both (FIG. 13-13). For accuracy and security against movement, clamp the two pieces down before cutting.

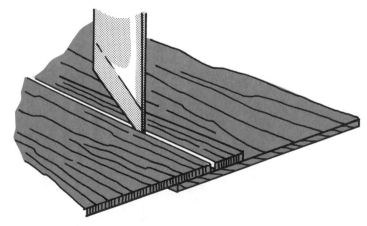

Fig. 13-13. Cutting veneers to match.

If you use a built-up patch, you can use masking tape or a special veneer tape on the surface over the joint to hold it until glued and set. It is a good idea to do this over all new joints. These tapes should peel without leaving marks, but if not, sand the tape away. Remember, the extreme thinness of the veneers and sand cautiously, or you might need to repair your repairs!

It is sometimes difficult to keep veneer in position during repairs. Veneer pins, which are extremely thin nails, can be driven just far enough to hold the veneer until the glue has set. Ordinary domestic dressmaking pins are just as good. When a pin is driven, it pushes fibers aside. It does not remove any wood. Consequently, it is possible to make a pin hole close again by swelling the fibers with water. Do not soak the piece particularly if you have used a water-soluble glue, but put just a spot of water over each hole and leave it for a few minutes.

Sometimes repairing veneers means replacing damaged cross-banding and the veneer adjoining it. Cross-banding is veneer that has a grain running opposite to the grain of adjoining veneer. Replace the adjoining veneer first, then cut off the surplus veneer (FIG. 13-14) and glue the cross-banding into place. If the cross-banding lies along an edge, leave some excess to be cut away after the glue has set (FIG. 13-15).

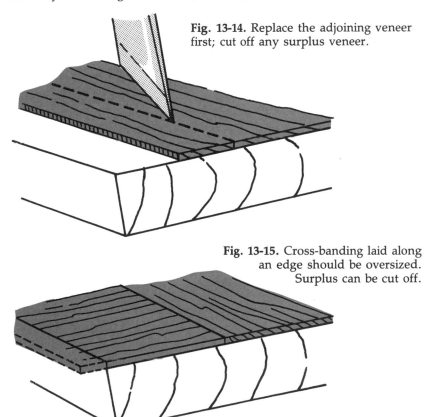

Fig. 13-14. Replace the adjoining veneer first; cut off any surplus veneer.

Fig. 13-15. Cross-banding laid along an edge should be oversized. Surplus can be cut off.

If the veneers on two different surfaces must meet, be careful not to undercut when trimming the first veneer. See that it is level with the other surface and does not fall away (FIG. 13-16). Then glue on the other veneer. Leave some surplus and trim that carefully (FIG. 13-17). Finally very lightly bevel the edge or slightly round it with just one stroke with abrasive paper. There is very little veneer overlapping on the angle, but if it is left sharp, it might catch and break away.

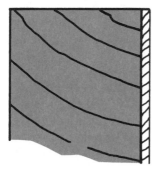

Fig. 13-16. Veneers laid on two different surfaces must be carefully matched. The first veneer laid should be flush with the second surface.

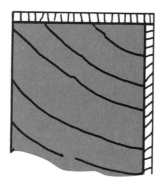

Fig. 13-17. Let the second veneer cover the edge of the first.

If veneer must follow a curve, it might be possible to spring it into shape, but even then it might crack if it has the grain crosswise. Breaking is less likely if you dampen the veneer. Allow the moisture to penetrate for about 10 minutes before bending the veneer. Then bind it and leave it curved until dry. When it is dry, glue it in place. Alternatively, apply glue and bend the dampened (not wet) veneer in place. Use an iron on it to dry out the moisture.

LAMINATED PLASTIC

Formica and other laminated plastics have much in common with veneer. Laminated plastics are much more durable than veneer, however. There is little risk of damage after laminated plastic has been glued down, and the surface usually lasts a long time.

There are tools you can use to cut the material to shape. You can also saw it and file or even plane it, although the plane will need frequent sharpening.

Although there are adhesives that allow movement after the plastic contacts the wood surface, the usual contact adhesive requires correct location the first time. It is also important to exclude air as the material is laid; working out bubbles of air after laying is nearly impossible. Because of this requirement, it is necessary to provide guides to position and lower the material into place.

In the usual tabletop, with the laminated plastic going to the edge, place temporary blocks projecting above the surface as guides (FIG. 13-18). Then press the plastic against them and lower it in a curved sweep with one hand while the other strokes the surface down, thus avoiding pockets of air.

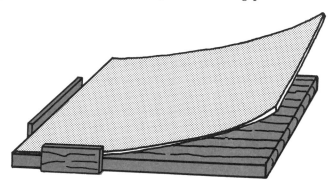

Fig. 13-18. Use blocks as guides for laying laminated plastic.

Patching laminated plastic is possible, but since there is no way of softening the impact adhesive, any part cut away might pull out wood fibers or leave uneven patches of glue. Before putting in a patch, therefore, you will need to level the wood surface so the new piece will become flush with the old surface.

An alternative is to put a new piece of the same material over the old. The same adhesive will work, but you should sand the old surface thoroughly so it will take the adhesive.

Putting laminated plastic around edges is very much like veneer edging. With the plastic, however, the bevel must be more pronounced: laminated plastic is thicker than most veneers. Usually such beveling leaves a black line between the two decorative surfaces, but this can be quite attractive (FIG. 13-19).

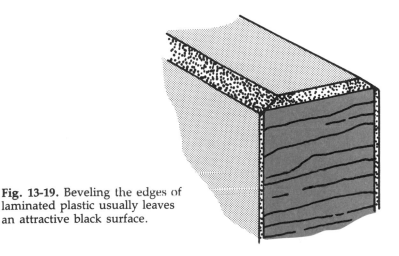

Fig. 13-19. Beveling the edges of laminated plastic usually leaves an attractive black surface.

14

Wood Defects

WOOD IS A NATURAL PRODUCT and is subject to defect. Man-made products can be produced with a uniformity of appearance and with durability; however, there is something lacking in these synthetic materials. In general, they do not have the beauty and character that wood has. So if you love wood, you must be willing to deal with its defects.

ROT

Attacks by fungi cause decay and rot. The effect cannot be reversed and there is no cure. Fungi are parasitic growths; some of them live on the organic matter in wood. Fungus seeds, or spores float about in the air and can settle on wood at any time, but moist conditions are needed for them to attack the wood. If the moisture content of the wood is less than 20 percent, there should be no attack. Fairly temperate conditions favor attack; attack is unlikely below freezing or in very hot conditions.

Fortunately, most furniture kept in normal room conditions will have less than 20 percent moisture content, but sometimes conditions are set up that invite attack. A liquid spilled on the top of a cabinet might leak to the inside, where lack of ventilation causes the moist conditions that enable fungus to become established. Nondurable woods (many of the softwoods and some of the hardwoods) are most likely to be attacked. A piece of wood that has both sapwood and heartwood in it might be attacked only in the vulnerable sapwood.

If a spore settles on receptive wood, it sends out roots, or *pyphae*, which spread through the natural cavities in the wood (FIG. 14-1). These roots take away cellulose from the wood, causing a complete breakdown of the character

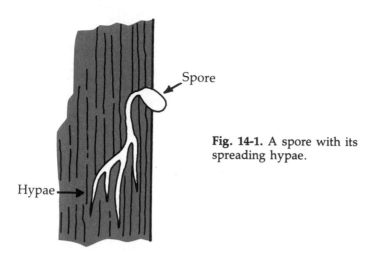

Spore

Hypae

Fig. 14-1. A spore with its spreading hypae.

of the wood. As the fungus feeds on the wood, it produces more spores, which are spread elsewhere in the same wood or carried by air, hands or tools to other wood.

Rot and decay can be divided broadly into dry and wet rot. The differences are not important to a furniture repairer. They both need drastic treatment. *Dry rot* is not aptly named because it can only occur in the presence of moisture and air. It flourishes in stagnant air. The wood changes color. Almost any color is possible, but generally, it becomes lighter in color than the overall tint of the particular wood. The wood will soften and lose weight. There is a musty smell. In an extreme case, the wood will disintegrate to a powder. If it has not gone as far, tapping the wood will produce a much deader sound at the rotted part than on the sound wood. The fungus looks like a soft, white spongy cushion.

The only treatment is removal of the rotted wood, which you should burn to destroy spores that can escape to attack other wood. Unfortunately, wood adjoining the infected area can carry live spores and hyphae, so you will need to cut away some good wood, too. The recommended cutting area is illustrated in FIG. 14-2. In some furniture of modest size, these distances are enough to enclose the entire woodwork and make the destruction of the whole piece advisable. Allowing active spores to remain in wood that is still receptive can only mean a spread of rot, with a risk to other nearby wood.

Since both air and moisture are needed for rot to develop, you should provide good ventilation for remaining wood. Any replacement parts should be of durable wood, preferably heartwood. Treat sound wood in the vicinity with a preservative, particularly if it is of the nondurable type. The spores can live on nearby objects of all kinds, so you must take precaution. A blowtorch flame played over masonry can kill spores. A solution of 4 percent sodium fluoride in water will sterilize masonry or metal.

Buying old furniture infected by rot is risky. Even if treated, it could bring spores into contact with other furniture and cause trouble there.

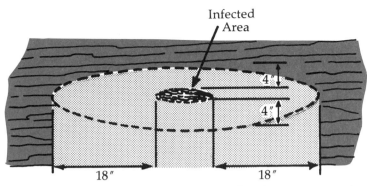

Fig. 14-2. The recommended cutting area for eliminating wood that can carry spores and hypae.

Avoiding rot is much easier than attempting to treat it after it has become established. Precautions to take are:

☐ Use wood with a moisture content below 20 percent. Most properly seasoned furniture wood is likely to have a moisture content of no more than 15 percent. Forced drying by heat is inadvisable because having wood too dry affects its workability and makes it brittle. Because dried furniture takes moisture again from the air to bring its moisture content up to normal (12 percent to 15 percent in room conditions), it can expand and distort.

☐ Ensure adequate ventilation. In most pieces of furniture that are normally dry there is little risk. Problems come if liquid gets inside or something is stored inside that gives off moisture.

☐ Treat new and surrounding wood with preservative while the wood is dry and before any surface treatment. Anything put on the surface, such as paint or varnish, will act as a barrier to the entry of moisture and might be adequate alone.

☐ Choose woods with a good resistance to rot. In a repair, this may not be possible because woods must match. Some woods resist attack by rot because of their chemical constituents. Teak and red cedar are examples. The manufactured woods have a resistance to rot. Particleboard has more synthetic resin than wood and should not be affected by dampness. Plywood has glue barriers that resist rot.

There are some fungi that attack wood while it is curing. At the furniture stage they might cause some discoloring or staining, but otherwise the qualities of the wood are unaffected. Discoloring in itself is not necessarily a sign of rot, so check for some of the other signs if you suspect rot.

BORERS

Rot is not a very great menace to furniture used in normal household conditions. A greater problem might come from insects. The damage is done by their larvae, which bore through the wood. There might be only small holes on the surface where entry was made, but under the surface there might be a maze of tunnels. (FIG. 14-3).

The tunnels might only be apparent after the wood is cut through. If the pupae are still active, you might be able to see cuts below the boreholes in certain seasons—early summer in the Northern Hemisphere. It is unlikely that furniture can survive a century or more without being attacked in this way, so there are likely to be worm holes in old furniture, although the piece might have been treated to kill the borers. Furniture fakers often drill imitation worm holes as some evidence of antiquity.

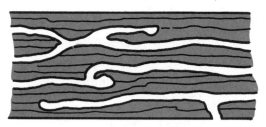

Fig. 14-3. Borers can weaken the structure of wood by tunneling.

The cycle commences with a beetle laying its eggs in a tiny crevice in wood. When the larvae appear from the eggs, they start eating the wood, boring farther into it for more food. This goes on for a long time, maybe a year or more. Eventually the larvae get near the surface and turn into pupae and eventually into beetles, which break out and the whole cycle starts again (FIG. 14-4). The beetles that cause the trouble might be no more than 1/8 inch long. Most of those that attack furniture in the home are about this size.

Fig. 14-4. The life cycle of a bore

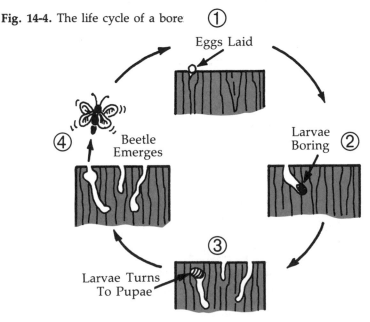

① Eggs Laid

② Larvae Boring

③ Larvae Turns To Pupae

④ Beetle Emerges

If there has been an attack by borers, you must provide a thorough application of an insecticide. Some common fluid such as kerosene, benzene, and turpentine may be used, but it is better to use a specially compounded commercial insecticide. Although there might be some benefit in painting on insecticide, sure results only come from injecting into individual holes. There are ways of ensuring good penetration by fumigation. This procedure must be done professionally, but a badly affected piece might be worth the expense of having it done.

Although particleboard is as immune to borer attack as it is to rot, plywood of some types can be vulnerable to borers. The larvae might not like the glue, but that does not stop them from burrowing through individual plies between glue lines. Older plywood, with nonwaterproof glue, is particularly vulnerable. Drawer bottoms and cabinet backs made from old plywood might be the home of borers. If these panels can be removed and burned, it is better to replace them than to treat them. Use plenty of preservative on the new plywood and the adjoining wood.

PRESERVATIVES

Fortunately, most of the furniture woods, particularly heartwoods, are unlikely to be affected by rot unless they are used in moisture-laden areas (like bathrooms or laundries). Although good home conditions provide some protection against borers, there is a risk of their attack almost anywhere.

Fortunately, preservatives can be applied to wood to give protection against both rot and borers. Some of them are for outdoor use, such as on fence posts and the exteriors of wooden buildings. They are unsuitable for furniture because of their appearance or smell. Tar oil products are in this group as well as some organic solvent types, such as chloronaphthalenes, copper and zinc naphthenates, and pentachlorophenol. There are also waterborne preservatives, such as copper or chrome arsenate, fluoride dinitrophenol, and sodium fluoride.

Furniture wood preservatives are available under trade names, and the small amounts needed in furniture repair are most simply obtained this way. In professional treatment, the preservative is forced into the wood. Alternatively the wood is soaked in the hot or cold preservative and then left for the liquid to diffuse through the grain.

These methods of application are not usually available or appropriate in furniture making and repair. You can provide sufficient protection by brushing or spraying preservative on. Of course, the preservative is only effective if it can soak in, so the wood must be clean and bare. Some preservatives affect the grip of glues. Therefore, it might be better to delay treating with preservative until after construction and before any finish has been applied. In many cases, some of the surrounding finish will have been removed as well, so this is an opportunity to treat old as well as new wood in the piece of furniture.

Surface treatments with polish or paint offer some protection against attack by borers, although obviously they only hide any action already taking place inside the wood. Quite often the hidden parts of the wood are without this protection, and their hidden parts might attract the beetle and her eggs. Treat these parts particularly well with preservative.

Be sure that the selected preservative is suitable for use on wood that will be painted, polished, or otherwise finished. The organic solvent types will take most finishes. Allow waterborne preservatives to dry; they will leave salt deposits on the surface. Wipe off the deposits cleanly. Then the surface can take paint, polish, varnish, or stain.

Most preservatives, other than the waterborne ones, are combustible during application. Some give off vapors that might be unpleasant, if not actually dangerous, when breathed, so application should be outdoors or in a well-ventilated place.

CRACKS AND KNOTS

As wood dries out, minute cracks in the grain might open. This problem often occurs after the wood has been worked and before the final finish. Sometimes, however, a crack does not appear until some time after the furniture has been in use. These natural cracks do not affect strength, so they only need to be treated for the sake of appearance. Normally, some form of stopping is used. However, just as the crack has opened, it might also close, so it is advisable to use a flexible stopping, not a rigid one.

Knots in hardwoods are usually unlikely to give trouble. In softwoods, however, a knot might dry out and shrink away from the surrounding wood; it might even fall out. Be suspicious of a knot in softwood that has a black ring around it. The knot almost certainly will weaken and fall out. Avoid using such wood in a repair. If a knot has fallen out of existing work, however, you can drill the hole to a true circle and insert a plug. You can plug a small knot with stopping. Expect a softwood knot on a surface that is to be painted to exude resin after the paint has been applied. Apply shellac to the knot to prevent resin from breaking through the skin of the paint.

15

Rebuilding Furniture

MANY PIECES OF FURNITURE can be restored and given a new lease on life through minor repairs, touching up of veneers, or treatment of rot or borers. Much furniture that has been discarded by someone can be made attractive again with a little skill and a lot of patience. Sometimes, however, furniture needs, and deserves, more challenging repairs—repairs that involve rebuilding.

Do not rush into such a project. You must assess the damage and the amount of work involved, then determine the way it is to be accomplished. You might need to discard some joints, incorporate new parts, or match woods.

Rebuilding from a very badly damaged piece of furniture is a challenge, and only you can decide if it is worthwhile. It could mean a lot of work for a rather indifferent result. It could also be a very satisfying achievement. Although there is a lot of satisfaction in making a completely new piece of furniture, there are occasions when the charm of an old piece justifies the time spent restoring it.

PLANNING RESTORATION

The way to start is not to rush into the removal of damaged parts. Instead, check sizes and shapes. Compare opposing parts. In most pieces of furniture, there are paired parts. If one is badly damaged, the other might provide a guide to the shape of the replacement part. If not, you might need to make a drawing of what is left of a broken part before dismantling it. This can be on paper, but quite often it can be on a piece of scrap hardboard or plywood held against the part, which is drawn around. Make sure you have all the facts you need before you cut out damage or remove joined parts.

Check for symmetry. If a framed structure has loosened joints, it could have moved out of true. If there is any doubt, get the whole thing pulled together with bar clamps or ropes and check corners with a square. Measure diagonals, too. You will need to check these things at the final assembly, but testing now might show up distortion caused by a warped or broken part.

Whenever possible, try to fit replacement parts in exactly the same way as the originals were installed. This is not always possible because sometimes joints cannot be opened without damage to a part that is not to be replaced. If there are mortise-and-tenon joints, you should use them if possible in the new work.

Usually, even a simple restoration job involves several steps. It's always a good idea to think the steps through before starting. Let's run through the replacement of a chair arm. This should give you some idea of the kinds of things that must be anticipated. First, make cuts on each side of the old joint at the front; also make a cut close to the joint at the back (FIG. 15-1). Then make cuts around the front joint to expose the edges of the tenon. This will give you an idea of the size of the mortise and tenon. When you have defined the dimensions of the joint (FIG. 15-2), cut the rest of the arm wood away (FIG. 15-3). Look for any nails or other metal fastenings. If necessary, cut through them with a hacksaw. Quite often it is possible to cut away wood around them so they can be withdrawn.

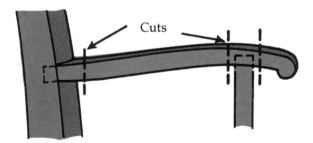

Fig. 15-1. To replace the arm of a chair, first cut off the old arm.

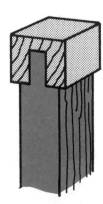

Fig. 15-2. Cutting around the joint helps to define its dimensions.

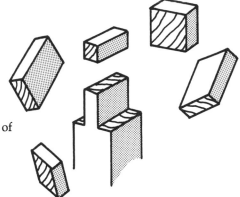

Fig. 15-3. Cut away the rest of the wood around the joint.

At the back, the outline of the mortise will be exposed (FIG. 15-4), with the wood on the tenon still inside. Remove some of this wood by drilling, but keep the diameter of the drill less than the width of the mortise (FIG. 15-5). Avoid going too deep. If there is a nail or other metal fastening through the mortise, cut it with a metalworking drill. It is then usually possible to lever or punch the ends out. Cut out the rest of the tenon wood, trying not to enlarge the mortise.

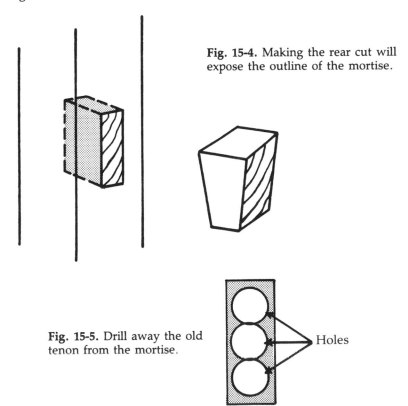

Fig. 15-4. Making the rear cut will expose the outline of the mortise.

Fig. 15-5. Drill away the old tenon from the mortise.

Holes

Make the new arm to match the opposite one. If the arm is shaped, use a piece of wood large enough to allow for the curves. Outline the shape of the arm on the wood. Outline in one plane at a time (FIG. 15-6). Cut along the outline in the first plane, then mark the shape in the second plane. Usually, you can cut the tenon as you cut the larger outline—one plane at a time.

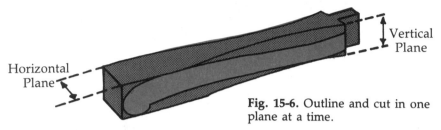

Horizontal Plane

Vertical Plane

Fig. 15-6. Outline and cut in one plane at a time.

Aim to make the joints tight. Duplicate the actual dimensions of the old parts, not the theoretical dimensions. If the upright tenon obviously started 1/2 inch thick but is now mostly thinner and rounded on the end, try to make the mortise match that shape.

Round and shape the arm, but leave final sanding (maybe even final shaping at clamp points) until after assembly. This method eliminates any marking as the parts are forced together.

PANELS

If you must replace a panel, the problem is to get it out with minimum damage to surrounding woodwork. It will either be grooved into the framework (FIG. 15-7) or held into a rabbet with molding (FIG. 15-8). If it is a glass panel or a wooden one covered with tapestry or other nonwood decoration, it will

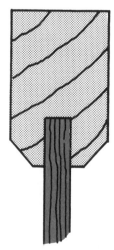

Fig. 15-7. Panels can be grooved into the framework.

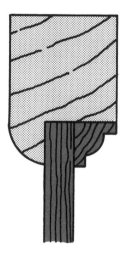

Fig. 15-8. Panels can be set into a rabbet joint braced by molding.

almost certainly be in a rabbet, although this fact might not be immediately obvious. The molding is unlikely to be glued, but will be held with a number of fine nails. They might not be easily seen, particularly if they have been punched and covered with stopping, which has been obscured by the subsequent finish. The loose side in the open rabbet is usually the side that has the least elaborate molding.

Sometimes, you can ease a wide chisel or a knife under the center of the molding to lift it. It should be possible to spring the molding sufficiently to release the nails (FIG. 15-9) and allow the miters to come away at the corners. When one length of molding has been removed, the others should come away with little trouble.

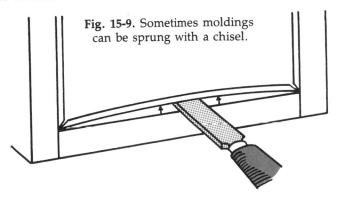

Fig. 15-9. Sometimes moldings can be sprung with a chisel.

The old panel should come out without difficulty. You can use it as a pattern for the new one. Be careful that the new panel does not distort the final assembly. You might need to duplicate any errors in the old panel. The original might not have corners at exact right angles, particularly if it is a very old piece of furniture. Forcing the framework to right angles might affect some other part of the total assembly. Carefully scrape out the rabbet to remove blobs of varnish or other finish, particularly at the corners, so the new panel will bed closely. Examine the treatment of the old panel. It might have been stained and polished before fitting.

Plywood and other plain wood panels, particularly in more recent furniture, are more likely to be in grooves. If you must remove a panel and fit a new one, you might need to cut away one of the surrounding pieces. One way of dealing with a damaged panel is to leave it in place and cover one or both sides with plywood or hardboard (FIG. 15-10).

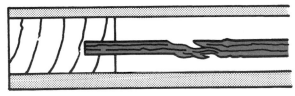

Fig. 15-10. Damaged panels don't always need be replaced. They can be covered over sometimes.

If you must remove the surrounding framework, look for fastenings that you can withdraw at a joint. These are unlikely, but if a joint is held by a screw, you might be able to open it. It is more likely that the corners will be solidly glued and have either mortise-and-tenon or dowel joints.

If the piece is old enough to have been made with animal or fish glue, you might be able to soften the glue enough to open the joints without cutting (FIG. 15-11). This can be done with heat. A gradual soaking in heat is better than applying great heat for a brief period. Leaving the joint close to a heat source for some time might be effective. Hot-water bottles tied over the joints for an hour or so might produce enough heat to weaken the glue. An alternative to heat is moisture. Soaking the joint in water should cause old glues to weaken to the point of allowing release.

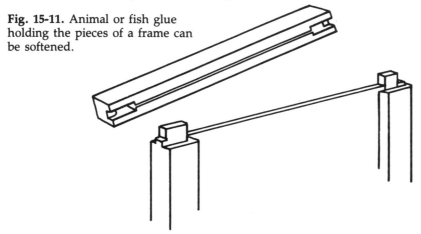

Fig. 15-11. Animal or fish glue holding the pieces of a frame can be softened.

Of course, a problem with the use of heat or moisture is that surface finishes might be damaged. If the piece is to be stripped for refinishing, this problem might not matter. If the existing finish is to remain, however, avoid heat and moisture.

Sometimes you can cut the joints of a frame surrounding a panel. At a corner, one piece usually abuts the other on the surface, and the workings of the joint might not be apparent. You can make an inconspicuous cut with a fine saw along the joint line (FIG. 15-12). If you cut two joints along the same

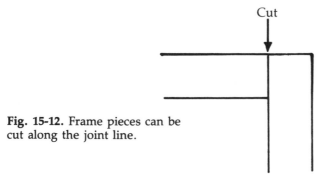

Fig. 15-12. Frame pieces can be cut along the joint line.

line in this way, you can remove the long piece and draw out the panel (FIG. 15-13).

In a door, it might be easier to make an inconspicuous repair by cutting out the bottom piece (FIG. 15-14), but this method will involve springing the frame a little to get the old panel around the ungrooved joint (FIG. 15-15).

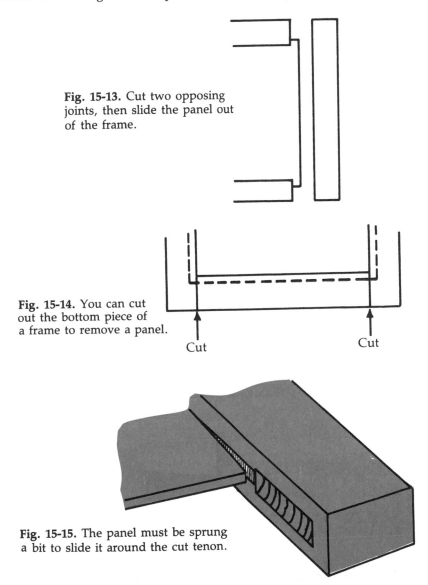

Fig. 15-13. Cut two opposing joints, then slide the panel out of the frame.

Fig. 15-14. You can cut out the bottom piece of a frame to remove a panel.

Cut   Cut

Fig. 15-15. The panel must be sprung a bit to slide it around the cut tenon.

If you remove the side of a frame then make and fit the new panel, you can remake the corner joints with dowels, preferably two in each joint (FIG. 15-16). You can make a jig to ensure matching holes (FIG. 15-17), or you can use an adjustable dowelling guide.

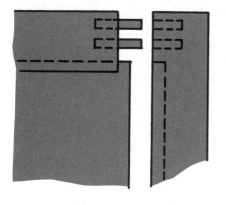 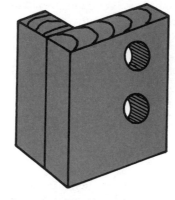

Fig. 15-16. You can remake the corner joints of a frame with dowels.

Fig. 15-17. Use a jig as a guide to ensure that the holes match.

If you remove the bottom of a frame, it would not be possible to use dowels of adequate length, even if the framework could be sprung enough. Instead, you can use open mortise-and-tenon joints because they will not show at the bottom edge of the door.

DRAWERS

If a drawer has been moved in and out for a very long time, there can be considerable wear on the meeting surfaces. In modern pieces of furniture, there are metal drawer slides, or the drawers might be hung with strips of wood sliding in grooves. Traditional drawers found in old furniture, however, usually have the bottom of the drawer itself sliding on guides. Some old drawers have kickers above (FIG. 15-18).

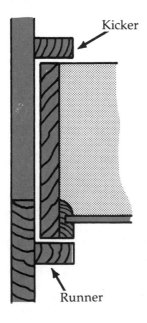

Kicker

Runner

Fig. 15-18. Kickers and runners act as guides for the movement of the drawers.

Wear occurs on the bottom edges of the drawer sides and on the runners. It is not usually difficult to remove the runners and replace them if worn, because they are often screwed in or are ready to break away.

If examination of the drawer sides shows that building up the worn part would be difficult, it might be preferable to increase the width of the worn runner and add a mating piece below the drawer (FIG. 15-19).

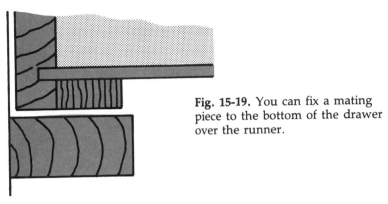

Fig. 15-19. You can fix a mating piece to the bottom of the drawer over the runner.

If there is enough depth below the drawer bottom, it is possible to skim off the worn surface that rides on the runner. Then you can add a new surface to mate with a new runner (FIG. 15-20).

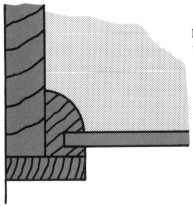

Fig. 15-20. A piece can be added to match the runner size.

Examine the top edges of the sides at the back of the drawer. If a heavily loaded drawer has been pulled in and out over many years, a surprising amount might be worn off the top of the sides because the weight of the contents tilting the drawer as it is pulled out (FIG. 15-21). You can inlay pieces to make up for this wear (FIG. 15-22), or in a bad case, glue on a full-length strip.

There may be a temptation to use a harder wood when repairing a badly worn part of a drawer or its runners and kickers, but a hardwood rubbing on a softwood will cause rapid wear on the softer surface. It is better to use

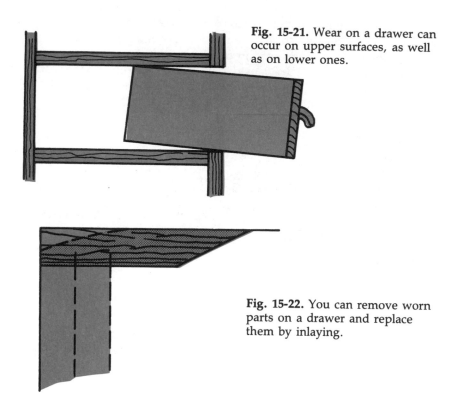

Fig. 15-21. Wear on a drawer can occur on upper surfaces, as well as on lower ones.

Fig. 15-22. You can remove worn parts on a drawer and replace them by inlaying.

the same kind of wood as previously used, especially if you are repairing an antique. You can reduce wear and ease movement of the drawer by rubbing the bearing surfaces with wax polish or candle wax.

LEGS AND FEET

Wear on old furniture often occurs at the points of support. Casters might wobble and wear away the wood, or the wood might suffer from direct contact with the floor. Legs, particularly at the rear of furniture, can suffer the attacks of borers without being noticed, and the wood can be so weakened that it will no longer support the furniture.

It might be sufficient to reseat casters by plugging the worn screw holes in the legs and rescrewing the casters in place, possibly with longer screws. Screw-on casters are common on older furniture, but modern pieces might use a type that has a stem in a hole in the leg. With an old piece of furniture, it might be better to replace the screw-on type with the stem type, if there is enough sound wood into which to drill a hole. Of course, the new type of caster must match the piece of furniture.

Another way of dealing with worn leg ends is to add a foot that will plug into a hole (FIG. 15-23). You can turn the foot from wood, or buy it in plastic or metal. Even on an old piece of furniture, such a new foot will be inconspicuous at floor level.

Fig. 15-23. Drill a hole in a leg end to allow a wooden foot to be plugged into the hole.

If a leg is badly worn or damaged, the only answer might be to cut away the bad piece and join on a new section. Where this is done depends on the design. It might be best to make the new part as short as possible. The new part might be less obvious if you bring the joint high enough to be under a shelf or rail. If the old piece is plain, a longer new piece might be advisable. If there is carving or shaping to be matched, however, it might be better to keep the new piece as small as possible.

In many cases, you can splice the new piece on, using a long diagonal cut. The new piece should be slightly oversize so you can trim it to an exact match after the glue has set.

There is an alternative that might be considered better for the downward load of a leg (FIG. 15-24). The V may point upward or downward, depending on which fits in with the design of the leg. This joint needs more care to make accurately. A simple splice is generally easier to make, so it does not show much when finished.

Fig. 15-24 New leg ends can be triangular.

RAIL JOINTS

Rails on tables and chairs can work themselves loose. Whether the rails are round, as in the underframing of chairs, or rectangular, there is likely to be wear both in the leg hole and the rail end. If rails are otherwise sound, it

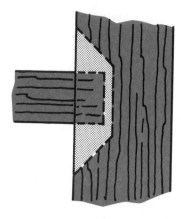

Fig. 15-25. New wood inlaid into a leg can take a rail.

might be advisable to keep them. Sometimes it is sufficient to reglue the joint using a synthetic resin glue filled with plenty of sawdust.

In a bad case, there are several options. You can fit a false tenon to the end of a rail, but it might be better to leave the rail end as it is and inlay a piece of wood in the leg. The piece of wood need not be much wider than the hole, but it should extend an inch or so along the grain in each direction. If possible, cut the wood with beveled ends (FIG. 15-25). Mark the position of the hole carefully before you glue the piece in.

HANDLES AND KNOBS

Handles, catches, knobs, and other such fittings can loosen with age and frequent use. Quite often they play an important part in the design of the piece and it would be unwise to replace them with something very different.

In addition to wear and damage to handles and knobs, years of handling might mar the surface behind them. So if you are restoring a piece, it is usually best to do something about the area behind a handle or knob also.

You can put a thin piece of matching wood behind a fixture and finish it to match the surrounding work. If you bevel or round the matching wood's edges, you will avoid a harsh shadow line. The matching wood need not be a simple rectangle, but you can shape it to match the handle or other features in the design (FIG. 15-26). The shape can also help disguise any repair if the door or drawer front has been badly worn.

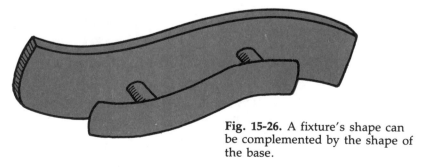

Fig. 15-26. A fixture's shape can be complemented by the shape of the base.

Sometimes screws in fixtures can work themselves loose, wearing away the screw holes in the process. No amount of tightening will correct this problem. It might be better to drill out the hole, insert a piece of dowel rod, and drill a new screw hole. It's best to use a washer under the screw head. The washer should be large enough to spread the pressure to wood that has not been pulled in (FIG. 15-27). You might be able to substitute a piece of metal or plastic tube for the drilled dowel.

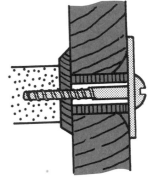

Fig. 15-27. A washer serves to spread the pressure exerted by the screw.

Another way of tightening the grip of the screw is to thread a piece of rubber tubing on it. The rubber tubing should be longer than the thickness it is to pass through. When you tighten the screw, the rubber will expand and fill the hole.

Damaged wooden handles are not such a problem. It is usually possible to make new ones of similar pattern. If the old fixing wood screws have worn their holes to a loose fit, you can make new holes and drive the screws in slightly different positions. If you need a backing piece to cover a shabby surface, you can make it to match the wooden handle.

Plastic and modern metal handles can be very attractive as replacement handles to cover a surface damaged by old handles. Obviously, most plastics would not be appropriate for a piece of furniture that dates before they were invented.

There were plastics used on furniture in the last century. Celluloid is an example. Therefore, at least some plastics can be appropriate for older furniture. Black plastic, used with restraint, would be acceptable for a complete handle or part of one, used with wood or metal. Clear or semiclear plastic, particularly with a tortoise-shell effect, might also be correct.

Some of the methods of plating metals are comparatively modern and it is safer to choose plain brass, which can be lacquered. Chromium plate and several other bright finishes would not be suitable handles on old furniture.

FIBERGLASS

An old-time cabinetmaker or a modern perfectionist might regard the use of fiberglass and its synthetic resin as inappropriate for furniture, but this and some moldable plastic substances might provide the only sensible way of restoring a piece of furniture. Some modern pieces of furniture are made completely from fiberglass.

The resins used with fiberglass will make a reasonable bond to wood, so it is possible to use fiberglass to repair wooden furniture. Fiberglass can also be bonded to fiberglass, providing the surface is sanded to expose new mat areas.

Fiberglass can be thought of as spun glass. When fiberglass (in a matlike form) is embedded in resin and dried, a remarkably strong material results. Layers of fiberglass can be built up in the resin to provide whatever strength and bulk is required.

Fiberglass is supplied in many forms. It is available as chopped strand mat, in which random short pieces of fiber are loosely bonded with an adhesive, which dissolves in the resin. This is the cheapest form and the type most suitable for many small repairs to wooden furniture. Fiberglass also is available woven in several ways into cloth or tapes.

The resin used remains liquid for at least several months after it is obtained, but it might be activated by the addition of one (sometimes two) chemicals. Once activated, it begins to set, and there is a limited time in which it can be used after hardening begins. For small repair work, a good way to buy fiberglass, resin, chemicals, and mixing containers is as a kit sold for repairs to car bodywork.

Carefully follow the instructions provided with the kit. Usually, you will apply the resin with a brush, using an up-and-down action after the first spreading. Cut the fiberglass to shape with scissors and lay in the resin, then introduce more resin with the brush. Permeation is indicated by the whiteness of the fiberglass changing to a clear appearance. If you need to use more fiberglass, you can put it on top and cover it with more resin. The first step in setting comes when the resin gels. If this happens in the mixing pot, it is too late to use it, and you should not attempt to spread it.

If fiberglass is to be bonded to wood, the wood must be absolutely bare. You should clean it of all paint, varnish, or other finish, then scrape and sand the surface so the fibers of the wood are exposed uncontaminated. The resin needs to soak into the pores of the wood, and paint or varnish in the wood might interfere with this process. Breaking up the surface by scratching or drawing a saw across it sideways should also provide a sufficient grip.

A fiberglass repair might be difficult to disguise, but such repairs can be done on the inside of furniture. Suppose a rail across the inside of a panel has broken under impact. It might be very difficult to replace. Bring the broken ends together as well as possible (maybe with glue against the panel) and cut off or fix down the worst of the frayed ends (FIG. 15-28). Remove all traces of finish from the broken part and the immediate area of the panel. Mix resin and paint thickly over and around the damage. It is a help if the work can be turned so gravity helps the resin flow where it is wanted and not away from it. If you must work with the furniture in a near vertical position, there

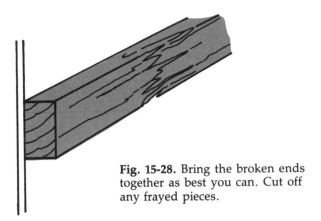

Fig. 15-28. Bring the broken ends together as best you can. Cut off any frayed pieces.

are thixotropic resins that resist any tendency to run. Place pieces of fiberglass mat or cloth over the break and allow them to overlap on to the panel. Then quickly brush on more resin to penetrate the fiberglass. Follow with more fiberglass, either the same size or slightly smaller, and enough resin to penetrate and cover it (FIG. 15-29).

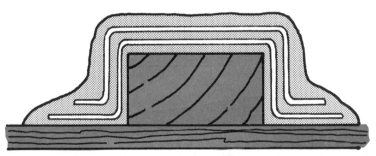

Fig. 15-29. Layers of resin and fiberglass are laid over the wood.

The actual thickness of a fiberglass repair is usually not very much, and it is possible to sand the result and paint over so it is not very obvious. This means fiberglass can be used on a visible surface of some painted furniture, like lawn chairs or workshop furnishings.

You also can use this method on internal parts that have come away from the main structure or on loose dividers. You must clean off the surfaces bare, and work the fiberglass into the angles with plenty of resin (FIG. 15-30). This may be done on both sides or only one. There might be more than one layer of fiberglass. Woven fiberglass tape is convenient for this kind of repair.

The resin suffers in the same way as synthetic glues if it is used without reinforcement. When fully set, resin will craze and lose much of its strength. There are, however, puttylike mixtures that contain particles of fiberglass mixed in resin. They are sold particularly for filling holes and dents in car bodies, but the material will also fill holes in woodwork. In making a fiberglass repair to a piece of furniture, any place that appears to encourage a buildup

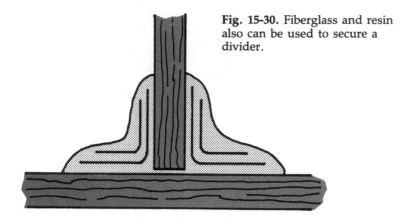

Fig. 15-30. Fiberglass and resin also can be used to secure a divider.

of resin without the mat or cloth reinforcement can have small pieces of fiberglass worked in to have the same effect as sawdust used with glue.

You can use fiberglass tape like a bandage to strengthen a cracked or broken piece. It might be too obvious in a prominent position, but you could repair a rear leg or a floor lamp in this way. Bring the split or broken parts together, possibly with resin in the joint, then put resin on the outside, and wrap the fiberglass tape around as you brush on more resin (FIG. 15-31). This method is suitable for square legs, as well as round parts. One overlapping wrap may be enough, but you can add another layer, either at the same time or after the first layer has set.

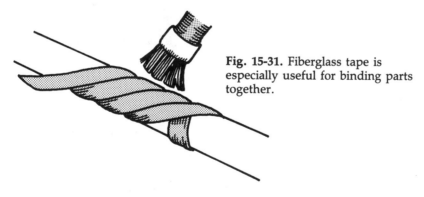

Fig. 15-31. Fiberglass tape is especially useful for binding parts together.

It is possible to build up a broken part with fiberglass and resin. Use resin and pieces of fiberglass and do a little at a time. Allow early layers to gel or harden, then add more. Under normal conditions and temperatures, the result should harden overnight, but strength and hardness builds up even more over several days.

If there is any surplus fiberglass and resin, you can trim it with a knife after the mass has gelled. After the result has hardened, you can saw and file it to shape. If a broken part has been built up, filing and sanding will work the repair to shape and leave a mat surface ready for paint. Not all paints are suitable for fiberglass, so check the instructions with the paint to see that the chosen finish is suitable.

There are other compounds available that will build up wooden parts and can be finished by filing and sanding. Although they come in colors to match certain woods, they are unlikely to become indistinguishable under a clear finish, so the best result will be by painting.

Fiberglass can be used in molding shapes too, such as for producing replacement parts. A simple example is a tray for the bottom of an umbrella stand (FIG. 15-32).

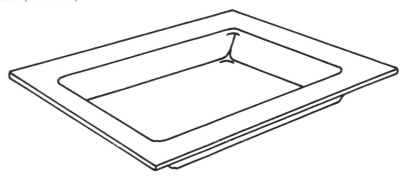

Fig. 15-32. A tray for the bottom of an umbrella stand.

First you must make a mold. For an elaborate project, there may first be a "plug" in the shape of the finished object. From the plug, make a fiberglass mold, then mold the production articles in this. For a simple object, such as the tray, you can omit the plug stage and make a mold straight away from convenient materials.

In the case of the tray, build up a block in the shape of the recess. This can be several layers of wood or particleboard, fixed down to smooth-faced hardboard (FIG. 15-33). The better the surface of the mold, the better the surface of the fiberglass.

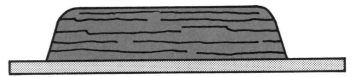

Fig. 15-33. You can make a mold from pieces of wood.

The next step is the coating of the mold with a *parting*, or release, agent. This is a wax compound that prevents the resin from adhering to the mold. Although you can use wax polish, it is probably wiser to buy a special preparation. Over the parting goes the first coat or resin. There are special "gel coat" resins for this purpose, but the resin supplied with a repair kit should be satisfactory.

Allow the gel coat to set. Then add more resin and lay in layers of fiberglass mat. You can cut pieces of mat to follow the shape, but adjoining pieces should overlap. Follow with a second layer of resin. This should be sufficient for our umbrella tray (FIG. 15-34).

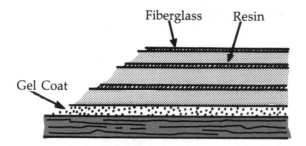

Fig. 15-34. A cross section of the fiberglass and resin layers.

Nothing has been done to restrict the outline, which will be ragged and uneven. When the whole thing has gelled, but has not become hard, trim the outline with a knife and straightedge or trim the edge later with saw and file. Leave the tray to harden on its mold for a day, then pry it off. Except for cleaning up the edges, it is finished.

16

Turning
and Carving

MANY PIECES OF FURNITURE have turned parts. Carving is less common on modern furniture, but much old furniture was carved, some of it quite elaborately. Both of these skills have been regarded as specialist trades, but anyone repairing furniture should not be afraid of turning or carving. These skills can be learned with practice.

Of course, a complete replacement of an intricately carved panel may be more than a beginner can hope to tackle, but straightforward turning and carving, particularly if it is only a part of an original that has to be replaced, can be very rewarding.

TURNING

A lathe is a machine tool. The machine rotates the wood, but the operator shapes it by hand. There are large lathes as well as much more basic ones that occupy little room. There are others that are just an electric drill that serves as a lathe. The method is the same; the main differences are the scope and the size of work that can be undertaken. The simplest lathes are suitable only for *spindle* work—anything round that is greater in length than in diameter.

A lathe has a headstock, which usually takes its power from a motor through a belt and pulleys (FIG. 16-1), but an electric drill on a stand can power the lathe directly. Earlier lathes were operated by a treadle, or, as they still are in some countries, by hand through a reciprocating action with a bow. The headstock holds the wood using a spur center. The parts of the lathe

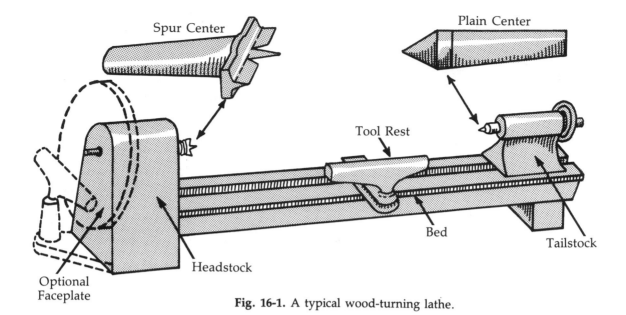

Fig. 16-1. A typical wood-turning lathe.

are normally on a bed (which might be two parallel metal or wood strips), a casting, or a large tube or rod. Sliding on the bed is a tailstock, which carries a plain center that supports the other end of the wood. The tailstock can be locked in any position on the bed, and there might be a screw adjustment for accurately positioning the center.

Tools are held in the hand, but they rest on a tool rest, which is usually T-shaped. Normally, the top of the tool rest is at about the same height as the center of the wood being turned. The simplest rest is fixed at this height, but a better one is adjustable and may have interchangeable rests. In any case, the rest must be movable so it can be kept close to the work.

A standard wood-turning lathe has no more parts than these. There is equipment for special purposes, but for ordinary turning, it is better for the lathe to be unobstructed. It is possible to do wood turning on a metal-turning lathe, but the slide rest and other complications interfere with the free use of hand tools. Also, wood turning throws wood chips in all directions, and there is soon a buildup of wood dust that will get into parts of the metal-turning lathe and interfere with its operation.

Most wood turning is done with gouges and chisels. Regular chisels could be sharpened to suit, but standard wood-turning tools are longer because there is sometimes an advantage in the use of length for leverage. A wood-turning gouge is grounded outside (FIG. 16-2). Some turners favor having it sharpened square across the end, but most gouges have their ends rounded. For small work, a 1/2-inch turning gouge will serve for general work, and a 1/4-inch one is good for smaller curves. Larger gouges are only used for large work, and even then their only advantage is in speed of working.

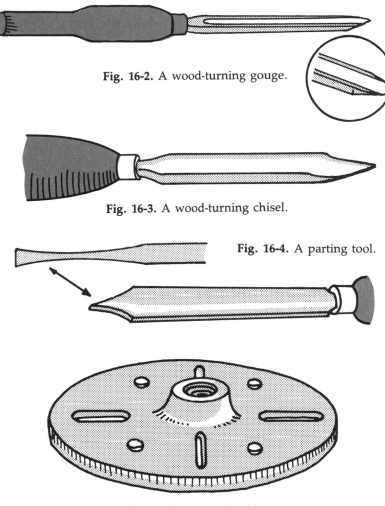

Fig. 16-2. A wood-turning gouge.

Fig. 16-3. A wood-turning chisel.

Fig. 16-4. A parting tool.

Fig. 16-5. A lathe faceplate.

A wood-turning chisel is beveled on both sides and is normally given a skew end (FIG. 16-3). Some turners prefer the end to be square across. A *parting tool* is a type of chisel sharpened across the end and narrowed behind the point (FIG. 16-4).

For larger-diameter work, the lathe may have a faceplate (FIG. 16-5) to which the wood being turned can be screwed. There are other chucks and holding devices that can be fitted to the mandrel nose (the driving part of the headstock). The maximum wood diameter that can be turned at the right-hand end of the headstock is limited by the height of the center above the bed, which might be cut away in some lathes to give a greater clearance. Some lathes are arranged to take another faceplate at the other side of the headstock (FIG. 16-5). With the tool rest kept out of the way, almost any diameter is

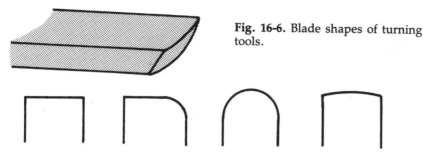

Fig. 16-6. Blade shapes of turning tools.

possible, and the limitation then is more likely to be the ability of the motor to turn the wood.

For turning between the centers, the grain of the wood is usually lengthwise. For turning disks, however, the grain must be crosswise. For bowls and similar objects, the tools used have more of a scraping action. They are thick and have flat-section obtuse scraping ends. The blades may be straight or curved (FIG. 16-6). These scraping tools are available commercially, but are often made by grinding old files.

Using Wood-Turning Tools

Wood to be turned between centers can be square, although some workers prefer to plane off the corners (FIG. 16-7). Mark the centers of the end of the wood with a center punch, and give the driving end for spur center a saw cut. Press the wood or slightly hammer it onto the driving center. Then bring the tailstock up and lock it to the bed. Adjust the tailstock so the center enters the wood. Apply a little lubricant and move the center further into the wood until it obviously holds it without vibration. Bring the tool rest close and check its clearance by pulling the wood around by hand before switching on the motor.

Bring a gouge squarely to the rotating work. Use one hand to hold it down on the tool rest, and keep the other near the end of the handle. You will need to experiment with the angle the tool approaches the wood at because this is affected by the height of the rest. If the handle is held too high, the edge only scrapes. As you lower the handle, you will reach a point where the edge slices off shavings (FIG. 16-8). Move the tool rest in as the diameter is reduced.

First, round the wood over its whole length with a gouge. You might need to make a succession of cuts inward, but once the more angular parts have been removed, you can draw the gouge along the rest to make more of a slicing cut (FIG. 16-9).

General shaping is done with the gouge. Work hollows from high to low, going down from the greater diameters, rather than up from the small ones (FIG. 16-10). Although the wood looks good while rotating, stopping the lathe will show that quite a rough surface is left from the gouge. This is purely an exercise for removing the bulk of the surplus wood. Do not take any part right down to size.

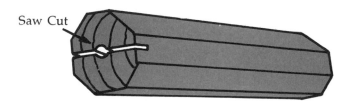

Saw Cut

Fig. 16-7. Turning can be easier if you plane off the corners of the wood.

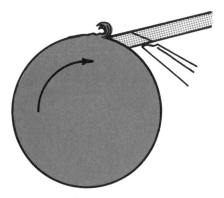

Fig. 16-8. Lower the gouge onto the turning wood until shavings appear.

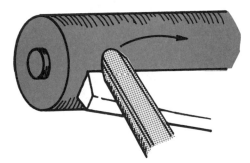

Fig. 16-9. Use a gouge to round the turning wood from end to end.

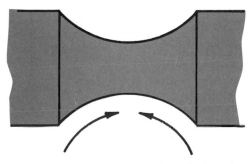

Fig. 16-10. Cut the hollows from high to low.

If you tilt a gouge toward the direction of cut, it will slice along the wood so the quality of the surface is improved. In some work, sanding after this procedure might be all that is needed, but a good surface is normally the result of work with a chisel.

There is not much risk of damage to the wood from using a gouge. At worst there might be a rough surface, as a result of scraping instead of cutting. More care is needed with a chisel; its misuse can cause it to dig in and spoil the wood. A chisel is used with a slicing action. Hold the chisel so the lower corner of the blade is presented to the work, allowing the point to slice (FIG. 16-11), moving along the wood lengthwise. To avoid digging in, keep the far side of the cutting edge well clear of the surface of the wood. In following a curve in profile, always make cuts from large to small diameters, with cuts meeting at the center of a hallow (FIG. 16-12). For heavy work, the hand on the tool rest might be fist upward, but for more delicate work, progress is more easily seen if only the thumb is on top.

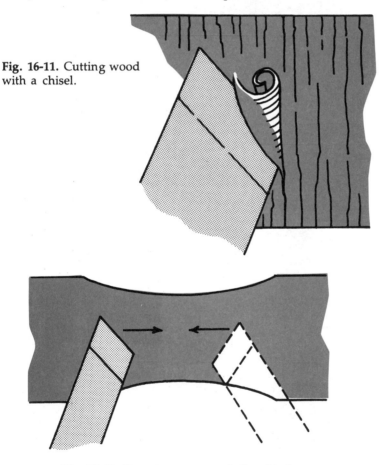

Fig. 16-11. Cutting wood with a chisel.

Fig. 16-12. To cut curves, work the chisel from the small diameters to the large.

With all turning tools, it is necessary to hold on very tightly. There is a natural tendency to hold tools lightly when making light cuts, but this should be resisted, otherwise the tool might kick back or twist and damage the wood.

When a chisel is used correctly and has a sharp edge, it will leave a surface as good as that from a plane. To reduce the risk of the point digging in, use as wide a chisel as is reasonable. Narrower chisels are needed to follow small curves, however. For repair work, nearly everything can be done with a 1/2-inch chisel. For large parallel surfaces or broad sweeps, a 1-inch or wider chisel is better; a 1/4-inch chisel will have limited uses in finer work.

The parting tool is used for squaring ends and for cutting straight into the wood to remove a waste end. Point it straight at the work, usually level at first; then lower the hand on the handle so the tool cuts, not scrapes (FIG. 16-13).

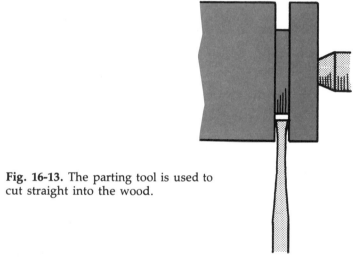

Fig. 16-13. The parting tool is used to cut straight into the wood.

Job Sequence

The sequence of tool operations is very important. Let's take a small replacement spindle as an example. If the spindle must match other spindles, you can use a marked piece of wood or card as a guide (FIG. 16-14). Use calipers to check these and other diameters.

Have a piece of suitable wood an inch or so too long. Round it on the lathe. Use a gouge to reduce it to close to the maximum finished diameter. Square the end next to the tailstock center by using the parting tool or by cutting in with the long point of a chisel (FIG. 16-15). With this cut as a guide, you can use a pencil on the rest to mark main cuts. Cut in main cuts with the long point of a chisel.

You can make the dowel at the tailstock end now, but it would be inadvisable to reduce diameters at both ends before working on other cuts: the wood could spring under the pressure, producing a distorted or rough

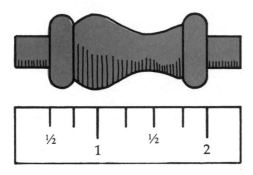

Fig. 16-14. Mark the dimensions of the spindle on a piece of wood or cardboard. Use the markings as a guide.

Fig. 16-15. Squaring can be done with a parting tool or the point of a chisel.

shape. Cut in with the parting tool or by successive cuts with a chisel as the wood is reduced. Remove the waste wood with a gouge. Then cut the dowel size with a chisel (FIG. 16-16). Since the dowel will need to fit a hole, check it carefully with calipers or use a hole in a piece of scrap wood to try over the end of the dowel after withdrawing it from the tailstock. For ease of entry into the final position, taper the end of the dowel slightly.

Narrow rounded parts, called *beads*, are found in much turned work. To make a bead, use a chisel that is little more than half the width of the bead. Hold the chisel with its bevel against the wood, its lower corner toward the direction it is to cut. Then roll the chisel so this corner cuts in, toward where the line marking the limit has already been cut in with the long point (FIG. 16-17). Turn the chisel over and do the same to the other side of the bead (FIG. 16-18). After practice, many small beads can be cut in one smooth sweep, but a more cautious approach with many light cuts is better at first, then do the other shaping, mostly by slicing cuts with a chisel.

You can reduce the other dowel to size in the same way as the first one, except you must cut in its end. Do not make the parting tool cuts much ahead of gouge cuts. If parting tool cuts are made much below the dowel size before any of the waste has been removed, the whole piece could snap during turning. It might be necessary to remove some of the waste part of the wood to allow easy use of tools (FIG. 16-19).

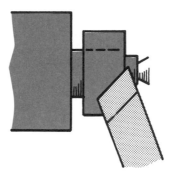

Fig. 16-16. The dowel can be cut to size with a chisel.

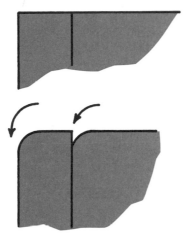

Fig. 16-17. Roll the chisel to round the wood.

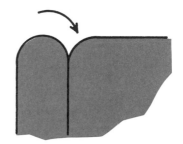

Fig. 16-18. Roll the chisel over the other side of the bead.

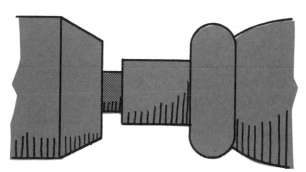

Fig. 16-19. If necessary, remove some of the waste wood so you can get at the dowel.

An expert turner is proud of being able to produce a tool finish that requires little or no sanding, but the revolving wood in the lathe lends itself to easy sanding. Poor tool work can be made good by using a fairly coarse abrasive. A coarse abrasive can also make prominent scratches around the work, however, and therefore across the grain. Use abrasive paper no coarser than needed, then follow with even finer grades so abrasive marks around the wood are too fine to be seen.

You can cut off the spindle with the parting tool, although there is always a risk of the final small part snapping and leaving a ragged mark. For a dowel going in a hole, a broken end might not matter, but elsewhere it might be better to remove the work from the lathe and saw off the last small diameter piece.

Turning Disks

For turning a disk-shaped piece on a faceplate, first cut the wood round with a band saw. The wood could be screwed directly to the faceplate with wood screws through the slots, but it is more usual to use a backing piece between the wood and the faceplate (FIG. 16-20). You can sandwich the backing piece between the wood and faceplate with screws or, once the backing piece is screwed to the faceplate, you can glue the wood to the backing piece (with paper in between). After turning is finished, you can break the wood away with a chisel.

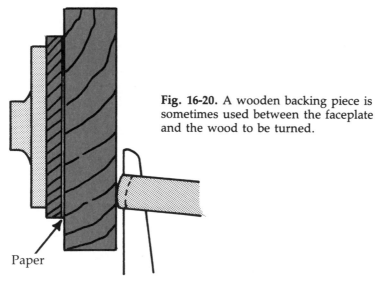

Fig. 16-20. A wooden backing piece is sometimes used between the faceplate and the wood to be turned.

Paper

Although some disk turning can be done with a gouge, it is more usual to do it all with scrapers, which are either used level or tilted slightly downward to the position that gives the best cut (FIG. 16-21).

It is usual to turn the outside of a disk to a true circle and then skim across the face to get a good surface. The next step—whether to work on the rim

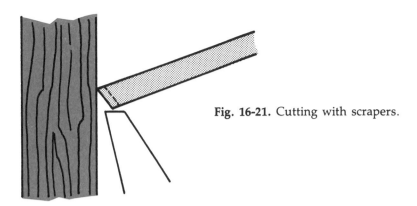

Fig. 16-21. Cutting with scrapers.

or on the surface—depends on what is being made. You can bring a bowl approximately to shape outside, then do the bulk of the hollowing. After that, you can finish the outside before getting the inside to the desired shape. For a lamp base (FIG. 16-22), rough out the general profile, shape the outside, and pencil in key points on the revolving wood.

Fig. 16-22. The cross section of a turned lamp base.

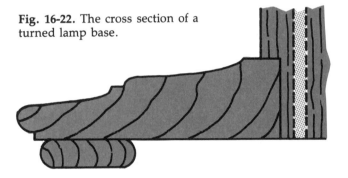

You will need to cut any angles in the disk with the square corner of a scraper tool or the long point of a chisel. Most other turning, whether roughing to shape or finally turning, is best done with a scraper tool having a moderate curve on the end. Place the scraper on the rest, which is kept close, and swing the tool in a series of small arcs (FIG. 16-23).

If a hole is needed at the center of the disk, you can make it in the lathe. Start a hollow with the corner of a tool (FIG. 16-24). If the wood is being turned over the bed and if the tailstock will take a chuck, you can use a drill. This is impossible in many simple lathes and would be impractical if turning at the other end of the headstock. It is possible, though, to turn the hole with the chisel. Use a chisel no wider than about three-quarters of the size of the hole and feed it straight in (FIG. 16-25).*

---

*For more details on wood turning, refer to *The Woodturner's Bible—2nd Edition* (TAB #1954) by Percy Blandford.

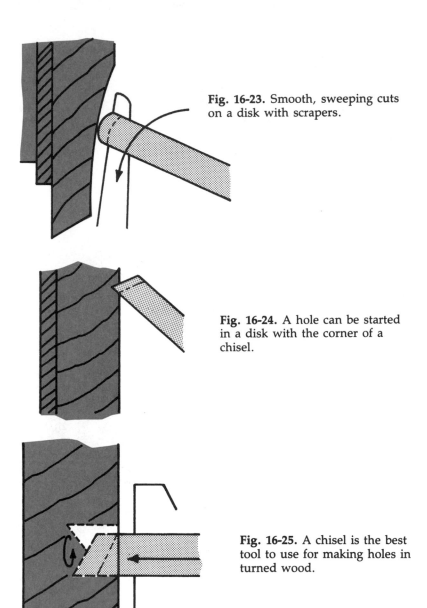

Fig. 16-23. Smooth, sweeping cuts on a disk with scrapers.

Fig. 16-24. A hole can be started in a disk with the corner of a chisel.

Fig. 16-25. A chisel is the best tool to use for making holes in turned wood.

CARVING

If carved work has been damaged, you will need to examine the state of the work to determine the best way of carrying out a repair. In many cases, it might be better to cut away much of the old carving so the joint between old and new will be less obvious. If the glue line can come along an existing line in the design, it might be nearly invisible. A joint that is in a recess will be less obvious than one on high surfaces.

It is easier to get a close fit with a straight joint, but sometimes it might be advantageous follow the moderate curve of some part of the carving (FIG. 16-26). Attempting to follow an intricate cut is inadvisable unless you are prepared to spend a lot of time exercising considerable patience and skill. With most carving on furniture, breaks or damage are most likely to occur at edges, so repairing is usually done by gluing on new wood and carving it to match after the glue has set (FIG. 16-27).

Fig. 16-26. Sometimes repairs to carved wood must follow curved lines.

Fig. 16-27. Fortunately, most repairs to carvings are done along the edges.

With some old furniture, the original craftsman showed his skill by doing fairly fine carving in depth, so comparatively fragile pieces projected high above the base surface. These projections might break off. To make a repair, inlay a piece of sufficient thickness and carve it to match (FIG. 16-28).

A difficulty with repairs to carving might occur in matching wood and grain. Check the direction of grain on the damaged part before cutting it away and replacing it. Grain will usually be lengthwise in the direction needing greatest strength. The wood might have a curved or wandering grain to follow the lines of carving, so the greatest success in a repair would be in using wood with similar grain pattern. This is not always easy and you might need to compromise.

Wood for carving should be without flaws. Any sign of a crack should cause the piece of wood to be discarded. Unless the original had knots or other flaws that have to be matched, it is better to use wood with a *mild grain*; that is, wood with an even grain pattern with no radical twists in the grain

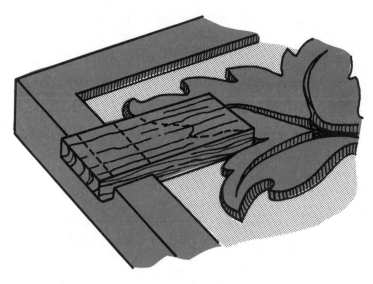

Fig. 16-28. Sometimes pieces must be inlaid before carving can begin.

lines. It will probably be easier to carve wood with little contrast in the grain colors than to use wood with prominent grain markings, unless prominent grain is necessary for matching purposes. Carving cuts have to be made in many directions, and there is less risk of tearing out in wood in which the grain lines have little prominence.

The traditional wood carver used a very large range of tools, most of them gouges. Antique carved furniture was worked with the facility of this great range. Fortunately, most repairs to carvings can be done with a few woodworking chisels, some woodworking gouges, a router, and a power saw.

Obviously, no repair should leave evidence of power tools. In some work, however, power tools can lessen the labor by taking the wood almost to size, leaving only light finishing cuts for hand tools. For instance, a router can take a background down to a uniform depth, then work with gouges can remove a further 1/16 inch to leave the hand-carved look.

Of course, much carving can be done with general woodworking chisels and gouges. This is particularly so with the bolder type of carving done in more recent years. Earlier carving was more intricate; finer carving tools are more appropriate for imitation of this kind of work.

The larger number of tools in the original carver's tool chest was due mainly to the great range of sweeps or curves in each width of carving gouge, going from near flat to deeper than semicircular (FIG. 16-29), with probably eight intermediate sweeps. Common carving gouges are straight (FIG. 16-30), but they might be curved (FIG. 16-31) to get into hollows, or spooned to get into smaller hollows (FIG. 16-32). A carving tool maker might still produce most of these tools, possibly only to special order, but there are smaller sets available. For repairs, it is probably advisable to accept one of these sets as an expert's selection of what is most likely to be required.

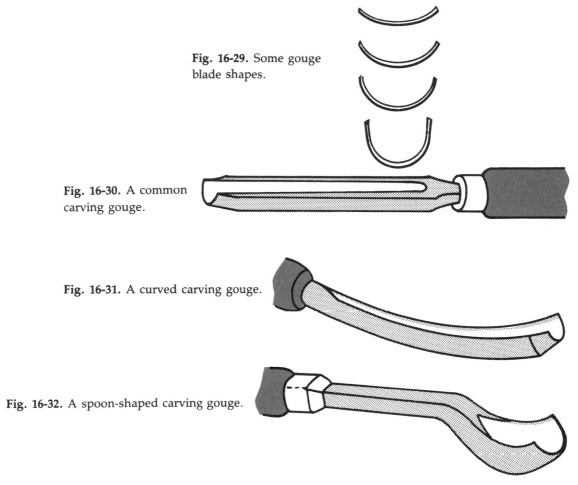

Fig. 16-29. Some gouge blade shapes.

Fig. 16-30. A common carving gouge.

Fig. 16-31. A curved carving gouge.

Fig. 16-32. A spoon-shaped carving gouge.

Other tools with gouge ends have been made, with the body of the tool curved in different ways or reduced in size to get into hard-to-reach places. If you have an opportunity to obtain old tools of this type, they are worth having, but they are not the sort to buy just for repairs.

Carving chisels are thinner than regular chisels and can be sharpened on both sides, with the greater bevel to one side. The end can be square across or slanted. Traditional carving involves fine grooves and lines. A narrow gouge, called a *veiner*, cuts lines like the veins of leaves, hence its name. It is possible to cut a V-shaped groove with a chisel, but there are parting tools available in several angles and sizes that can also make a V cut (FIG. 16-33).

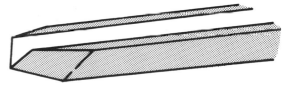

Fig. 16-33. The blade of a parting tool.

It is important to keep carving tools sharp. While outside honing can be done on an ordinary oilstone, sharpening inside calls for slipstones, which are used like a file on inside surfaces. A slipstone with a round edge and

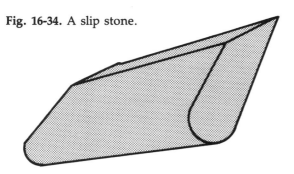

Fig. 16-34. A slip stone.

a chisel-shaped edge (FIG. 16-34) can get inside gouges and V-shaped tools. If there are many different gouge sweeps, however, you might want to have two or more stones that approximate the curvature of the sweeps. For the best sharpening, it is worth having two grades of stone; a coarse one will quickly remove metal, and a fine one will produce a good edge. For ordinary chisels and gouges, it is usual to sharpen tools with a flat surface opposite the beveled one, but a carver likes to have a slight bevel on the second side.

Anything being carved should be held securely. Both hands should control the tool, so fix the wood to a bench, unless it is so massive that it will not move. You can use clamps, bench holdfasts, and vises. For most carving work, it is necessary to arrange the surface being carved so that the tool can be brought to it from any angle without obstruction. It is usually best to have the surface slanting upward but this is not always possible.

You can do much carving with hand pressure. One hand should ride on the tool handle to provide pressure and control. The other hand should ride over the blade, assisting in control but ready to provide restraint if the tool tries to go ahead too far or too fast because of the softness of the grain. For fine work and the greatest control, use hand pressure, particularly where new work adjoins existing carving.

For harder woods or deeper cuts, you might need to hit the carving tool with a mallet. There are special round carver's mallets, but any available type is suitable. Hold the carving tool in one hand with the fingers around the handle and the thumb toward the end being hit by the mallet. The wrist or arm should rest on the wood or somewhere else solid so the carving-tool direction can be controlled. Mallet blows should be frequent and light, rather than heavy, to control progress.

For most cuts, the corners of the tool should be above the surface (FIG. 16-35). If the final shape is deeper than the tool, work it down with several cuts. Avoid burying the corner of a tool to reduce the risk of splitting. Sometimes breaking away waste wood is intentional, then a tool might have a corner entering below the surface (FIG. 16-36).

Carving often must be done in all directions, but if you understand the grain and cut accordingly, a smoother finish will result and there will be less risk of the wood breaking out. You can think of lines of grain as pieces of straw. An upward-sloping cut will shave the ends off (FIG. 16-37), while a

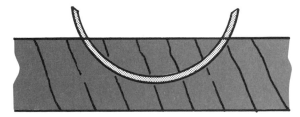

Fig. 16-35. In carving, the upper edges of a gouge must ride above the wood surface.

Fig. 16-36. If you want to break away waste wood, dig into the surface with the corner of a gouge.

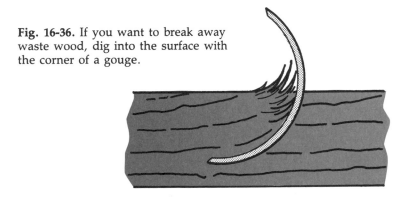

Fig. 16-37. If possible, work across the ends of the grain in an upward-sloping cut.

downward-sloping cut might bend the ends over (FIG. 16-38) and either cause splits or a ragged end. Therefore, use an upward sloping cut even when cutting across the grain, going diagonally up the slopes of grain rather than down. A sharp tool is much less likely to cause the grain to break out than a blunt one, and you can make slices across the grain with a sharp gouge with confidence so long as you keep the tool corners above the surface.

An attraction of carving is the way it gives a three-dimensional look. Good carving on furniture will often appear to be much deeper than it really is. The sense of depth is a result of the way the carving was done. Nowhere on the carved part is there any flatness. When carving such a panel, none of the original surface should remain as it was before carving started, even if all that has been done has been some light cutting using a gouge with a shallow curve. Prominence is given to a part by undercutting; the shadow will make the wood above stand out (FIG. 16-39). Of course, undercutting could weaken the carving, so avoid excessive undercutting.

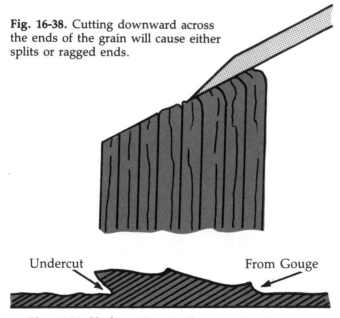

Fig. 16-38. Cutting downward across the ends of the grain will cause either splits or ragged ends.

Undercut   From Gouge

Fig. 16-39. Undercutting emphasizes raised areas.

The first step after marking out a design is usually to cut away the background by outlining it with a deep gouge and cutting across the grain toward the outline (FIG. 16-40). If there is no need for undercutting, the edge of the raised part is stronger with the curved edge left from a gouge.

With the background lowered, the remaining raised part is where most of the carving usually occurs. If the repair is part of a repetitive design, there will be guidance elsewhere on the furniture. Laying a straightedge across parts of equal depth will show you how deeply to cut certain parts. Even if there is not an identical pattern elsewhere, the general arrangement of the

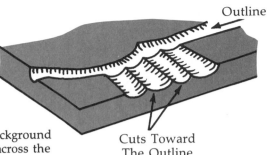

Fig. 16-40. Outline the background first. Then cut toward it across the grain.

design will show you how deeply to cut. Cut in broad sweeps, not in hesitant, light jabs.

If there are leaves or foliage to be cut, there is no need for machinelike duplication of each part. Nature did not make the originals all alike. A leaf has curves all over, some upward and some downward. Sweep your gouge around to get the general effect (FIG. 16-41) before you cut in veins and other details. You can make a leaf or any other object look deeper if its surface is not level with the general plane of the wood. Instead, undercut the high part, and this part of the carving will stand out more than if left near flat.

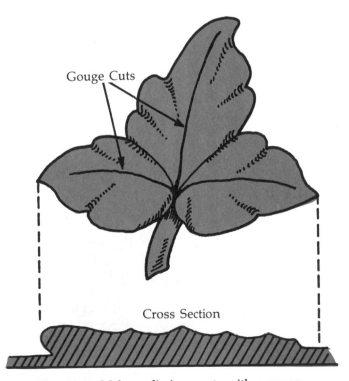

Fig. 16-41. Make preliminary cuts with a gouge.

Chip Carving

Some early furniture was decorated by chip carving. The only tool used was a knife. In most repair work, chip carving will consist mostly of a series of triangles cut in patterns (FIG. 16-42).

In the basic triangle, lines from the center to the corners are cut with a knife (FIG. 16-43). Then slices are made toward the center from the outline with a knife or chisel (FIG. 16-44). Sometimes there are curved lines, but the multiplicity of patterns found usually can be broken down into a large number of these triangles.

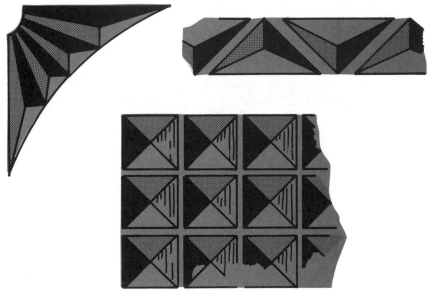

Fig. 16-42. Chip carvings.

Fig. 16-43. First cut from the center of the triangle to the corners.

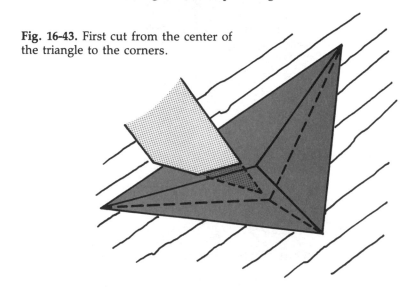

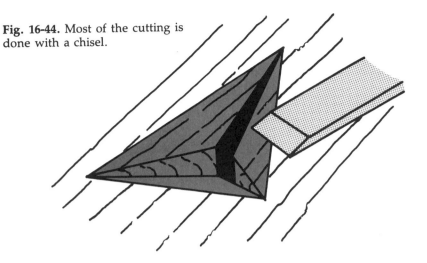

Fig. 16-44. Most of the cutting is done with a chisel.

Finishing

The old-time carver did all the work with his gouges and chisels. If repaired work must adjoin such carving, the new work should have a good tool finish. Sanding a carving alongside an unsanded part will usually make the repair look shabby. If the quality of tool work is not as good as was hoped, it is better to scrape a poor surface than to sand it.

You can use a cabinet, or hook, scraper, but you might need to make a special scraper to set into shaped and narrow parts. This is a piece of tool steel, of the type used in saw blades, and might be from a discarded hacksaw blade. Curve the end and sharpen it like a chisel, including honing (FIG. 16-45). Rub a burnisher (any hard steel) over the edge to put a burr on it. Hold this scraper in such a way that the burr does the cutting (FIG. 16-46).

Where the carved repair includes broad curves at an edge or other part accessible to large tools, it might be possible to use a plane. The surface might need further treatment by scraping or sanding, but you can obtain the general shape quickly.

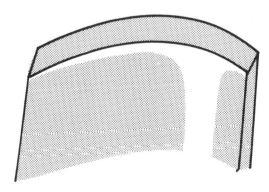

Fig. 16-45. The end of the cabinet scraper is sharpened like a chisel.

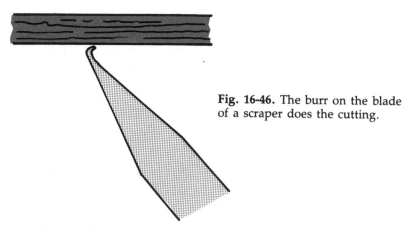

Fig. 16-46. The burr on the blade of a scraper does the cutting.

The intricacies of most carving make it very difficult to get an even finish by sanding because of the inaccessibility of some parts. This might not matter if the wood is left bare, but staining or lacquering might result in different coloring on sanded and unsanded wood. Check adjoining wood. The final finish might match better if none of the new work is sanded. Scraping will not affect absorption of the stain or finish as easily as sanding. In any case, only hand sanding is advisable. Any sort of power sanding is likely to lower high spots or cause flats where they are not wanted.

17

Upholstery and Seating

SEATING FURNITURE might have plain wood seats, which can be reasonably comfortable if shaped. For prolonged sitting and the greatest comfort, however, there must be some softening of the surface. This may be minimal and restricted to the part actually taking the weight. Part of the wooden structure might be visible, or the whole thing might be completely upholstered, with no wood showing except a few inches along the legs.

UPHOLSTERY

There have been many changes in upholstery materials and methods over the years. The way a repair is to be made depends on whether there is a need to maintain a semblance of the original work. Early covering materials were derived from wool or cotton and a few other natural materials. Leather was also used. Modern upholstery materials, which are often more durable, usually either are woven from man-made fibers or are plastics. Fortunately, many of the modern materials look so much like earlier materials that it can be possible to substitute them without spoiling the effect of an old piece of furniture.

Cushioning

New furniture usually has cushioning that is very different from that of old furniture. An old upholstered seat might have many layers of different materials. Canvas and muslin were used in addition to the surface material. Softness was provided by a variety of fillings. Feathers and down gave a flexible and soft seat or back, but horsehair, coir fiber, and many other fillers found their way into upholstery. Some of the materials used were not hygienic, and even if a traditional finish is expected of the repair, it might be better to change to modern, cleaner materials for the inside.

Nearly all new furniture has latex or polyester foam interiors. These are provided as cushions of various thicknesses, usually with hollows underneath (FIG. 17-1) or inside (FIG. 17-2). These cushions are available already shaped with square or rounded edges. It is possible to fix tape to them with adhesive, so a square edge can be pulled to a curve. If there are hollows on one side, the square edge will form a good curve (FIG. 17-3). The more solid cellular foam will pull to a curve better if cut at an angle (FIG. 17-4). Where cutting an edge exposes hollows that might show through the covering or affect comfort, you can use an edging strip (FIG. 17-5).

Fig. 17-1. Some latex or polyester foam cushions have holes on one side.

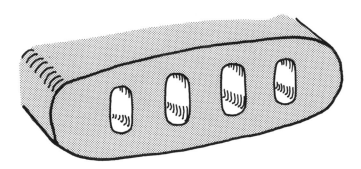

Fig. 17-2. Some foam cushions have holes on the inside.

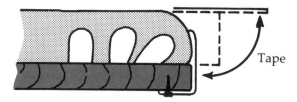

Fig. 17-3. You can tape down the end of a foam cushion to form a rounded edge.

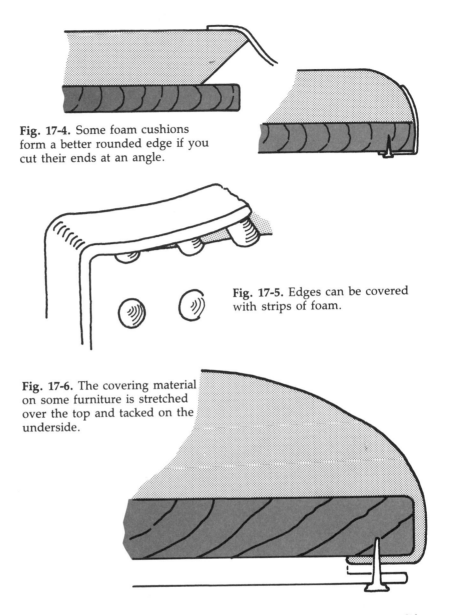

Fig. 17-4. Some foam cushions form a better rounded edge if you cut their ends at an angle.

Fig. 17-5. Edges can be covered with strips of foam.

Fig. 17-6. The covering material on some furniture is stretched over the top and tacked on the underside.

Chair and stool seats with only nominal softening often have a liftout panel fitting in a recess. The covering material is stretched over the top and tacked underneath (FIG. 17-6). For neatness there might be a piece of plain cloth stretched over the underside with its edges turned under.

What goes between the covering and the panel depends on the design. An old seat might have a few layers of cloth or something similar that has flattened almost hard with age. You can replace the filling with thin foam, if no more softening is required, or you can use a thicker pad of foam, with its edges curved, as already described.

Coil Springs

Much traditional furniture made use of coil springs. Some modern furniture also uses them. Some springs are supported on wooden framing, but usually they are braced by interlaced strapping or webbing. The traditional strapping was made from natural fiber, which eventually rotted or gave way. The only repair needed might be to replace this strapping.

A chair of this type usually has a coil spring at each crossing of the webbing, with a few stitches made with string to prevent the spring slipping out of place. You can cut away these stitches to remove the old webbing. The springs should remain attached at their other ends. Note the spacing of the webbing and mark its location, if this is not obvious, on the wooden frame.

Webbing, which is usually canvas, is fixed to the frame with tacks. If you must make a repair to the woodwork, it is advisable to use beech or other close-grained wood that provides a good grip for the tacks. When fixing new webbing, avoid driving tacks into old holes. Tack down the webbing at one end, with some surplus extending. Fold this surplus and tack over the first part (FIG. 17-7). A common arrangement is three tacks arranged in a triangle; the top is held down with three tacks arranged the other way.

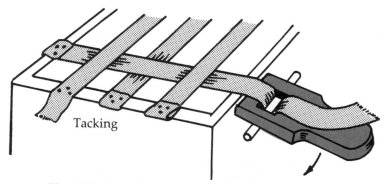

Fig. 17-7. A tool for putting tension on webbing.

Give the webbing a good tension using a lever, which you can buy or make (FIG. 17-7). This has a round end to bear against the framing and a hand grip at the other end. There is a slot wider than the webbing and a peg to push through a loop of webbing.

Lever the tool to get a tension, holding the surplus webbing by one hand, while you use a hammer to drive the three tacks. Next cut sufficient surplus off and fold it over the first tacks; then drive three more, as described before.

Although it is usual for the webbing in the two different directions to be woven over and under alternatively, this probably does not matter. What is more important is to secure the springs in place with string and a large needle. There are special upholsterer's needles, but you can use any needle with an eye that will take the string. Use enough stitches to hold the spring.

Knot the string securely, but do not make an unnecessary number of stitches; too many might weaken the webbing.

In some upholstery, the seating is suspended on a system of coils or other springs stretched across the frame. With foam cushioning above it, this method dispenses with the perpendicular coil springs and makes a thinner total section. Repairs might be necessary when springs break or come away from their fastenings. Since the springs are likely to be on the cushion side of the framing, you usually will need to lift the covering to get at the springs. The covering usually has tacks or nails, which you can pry away so you can turn back the covering to expose the foam, which you will need to remove to get at the springs.

There are several types of these springs, but failure might occur because the ends become unhooked. Simple hand tension might not be enough to get a spring back into place. If a cord loop is attached, you can use a lever to stretch the spring into position (FIG. 17-8). If springs have broken, not much can be done except replace them, which might mean a whole section if they are bonded together.

Fig. 17-8. Sometimes you must use a lever to get a spring back into place.

Strapping

Another method of support is the use of rubber strapping. This looks like webbing but is actually reinforced natural or synthetic rubber. Strapping is used on the surface next to the cushioning, which might lift out so that servicing the strapping is simple. The strapping might be fixed at the ends just as ordinary webbing is, but other techniques are also used, including the use of a groove in the woodwork. A metal clip is squeezed onto the end of the strapping to provide a rigid end to press into the angled groove (FIG. 17-9). If you need to fit new rubber strapping, you should use new end clips, although you might be able to remove an old end carefully, cut off the stretched strapping, and fit and end-clip again.

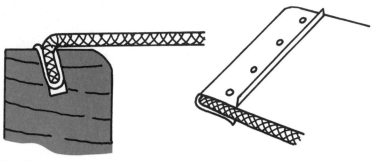

Fig. 17-9. Strapping can be easily fixed into a groove if it has a metal clip on its end.

Buttoning

With the older cushionings, there was a risk that they would move around if nothing was done to restrict them. This movement might have been prevented by the use of compartments, but buttoning was commonly used. Buttoning prevented a large area of padding from ballooning instead of remaining in shape, and it did something to stop movement of the filling. Although foam cushioning is in a form that cannot move around, it is still common to find buttoning, partly for the sake of appearance.

There is usually a top and a bottom button, joined with stout thread or string (FIG. 17-10). The top button has a loop at its back, while the bottom one can have two or four holes. Special buttons suitable for covering with chair material are available for use on the surface.

Fig. 17-10. Buttoning usually consists of top and bottom buttons.

There are long, double-ended upholsterer's needles intended for buttoning work. You must adjust the thread tension to give the right appearance on the surface. You can make the first experimental knot with the cushion compressed (FIG. 17-11). If this is satisfactory when released, tie the knot and work the thread around so the knot is hidden within the

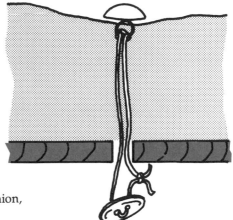

Fig. 17-11. Compress the cushion, then tie the knot.

cushioning. In some upholstery there might be a peg on the underside, instead of a button.

For the most durable repair, use a synthetic thread, so there will be no rot. Most synthetic threads are more slippery than natural fiber ones, so make sure the knot cannot slip. A *reef knot*, one with the ends half-hitched before cutting off, should hold (FIG. 17-12).

Fig. 17-12. A reef knot.

Covering Material

If cushioning or covering must be removed and replaced, inspection will show the sequence in which the work was done. Dismantling is in the reverse order.

On exposed parts, any tacks are likely to be covered with a tape, sometimes called *gimp*, which might be anything from a simple strip to a decorative piece with tassels. There are tack lifters with forked ends, but a thin screwdriver pushed under the head and twisted 90 degrees usually lifts the head enough to allow the use of pincers (FIG. 17-13).

Modern furniture makes more use of adhesives, so it might be necessary to break away old material that has been glued on. This doesn't matter if it is to be replaced, but make sure you understand the function of the particular piece and how it will have to be cut and reassembled.

You must arrange covering material so its main surface is evenly tensioned and any pattern is symmetrical. All other work on it is dependent on this. It is unwise to cut any exposed surface. Carefully fold corners.

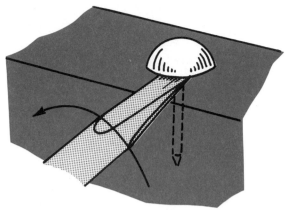

Fig. 17-13. Usually a thin screwdriver is all that's necessary to lift upholstery tacks.

If a curve must be followed or there is some other shaping, it is possible to avoid one large fold or crease by using a series of narrower tucks along an edge, each controlled by a tack. This method can be decorative. Do not try to trim the cloth to size in advance. Allow some excess around the edges to give you something to hold and pull while adjusting tension and fixing. You can do final trimming with a sharp knife.

There are now adhesives for just about every material. If you can find the right adhesive, you can put on a patch. It is difficult to make it inconspicuous, but if a hole has been made in an otherwise good covering, a patch might be preferable to an expensive, complete recover, at least for a short time.

On any tear or cut (under the patch) more than 1/2 inch long, sew a few threads across the patch to relieve it of tension. The arrangement of the stitches depends on the damage. Make a few large zigzag stitches on a straight cut; use a coarse darn on a more open hole.

The patch will stay down better if its corners are rounded. Sharp corners are the first parts that will lift away. Cut the patch so it matches the pattern. A circle or ellipse might be less apparent than any patch with straight lines (FIG. 17-14).

If the patch is a plastic imitation leather or other fairly thick substance, you can sand it down on the underside to thin the edges (FIG. 17-15). You can pare some material with a razor blade or knife.

Follow the manufacturer's instructions for the adhesive used on the patch. Avoid getting adhesive around the repair. Pencil in the shape of the patch and carefully spread the adhesive within the outline. On plastic surfaces, it is usually helpful to scrape the old surface with a knife just before spreading adhesive to get rid of dirt and grease on the surface and remove the oiliness present on the surface of some plastics.

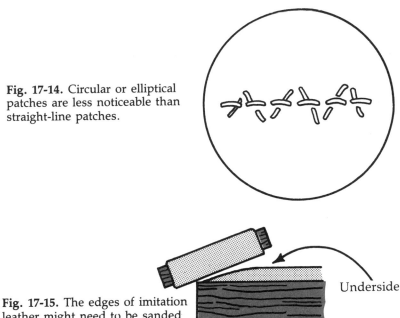

Fig. 17-14. Circular or elliptical patches are less noticeable than straight-line patches.

Fig. 17-15. The edges of imitation leather might need to be sanded on the underside.

Underside

RUSH SEATING

The alternative to a plain wooden seat or an upholstered one is a seat made of flexible material that provides its own cushioning. The country craftsmen in Europe and the pioneer settlers employed any material at hand. One result was the use of rushes in a configuration that has become known as a *rush pattern*.

Sedges and rushes grow in marshes and along river banks. There are several types, some of which are suitable for seating. At one time, locally available rushes were twisted and plaited so they could be used for baskets, mats, and other things, as well as chair seats. Probably the best type for seating grows in deep water and can reach 8 feet in length. This type is called the golden rush, or *bulrush*.

To be useful, rush must be twisted into a kind of rope. Most rush must be wetted as it is used. As a chair seat is built up, the rush is twisted in as needed. Having the damp rushes scattered around means you cannot work in a living room.

There are several rush substitutes. These are long, ropelike materials, so wetting and twisting as you progress is unnecessary. Consequently, the work is less messy.

The material nearest to rush in appearance is seagrass, which is rush colored. It is supplied in hanks as a two- or three-strand rope. Several thicknesses are available, and the coarser type is most rushlike in the finished seat. Similarity to rush might be important for reseating old furniture, but the finer grades might make a more interesting seat for modern furniture.

Never color rushes; they do not take dye well. Seagrass is available colored, which might suit your furniture color scheme, but would be inappropriate if you were trying to simulate rush.

Any type of rope can be worked into a rush pattern. Dacron or other synthetic rope can make an interesting seat on modern furniture. Natural fiber rope, with its more hairy appearance, gives a finish between seagrass and the synthetic rope.

Usually the fault that develops in an old rush seat is sagging, which develops into breaking of the rushes and a hole at the center. Rushes and seagrass are natural materials and will rot as they get old, but they have a long life if kept in a dry atmosphere. There is no satisfactory way of patching these materials, so when they wear out, you should cut them away and burn them.

You might need to remove a few nails or tacks in the rails. It is interesting to see how the rails of an old chair will show the marks of shaping with a draw knife. More recent furniture will have machined wood or be hand planed. In any case, reseating is an opportunity to sand the wood and reglue weak joints, as well as attend to the finish of the chair in general.

It is helpful to make a few wooden shuttles, on which to wind the seagrass or rope (FIG. 17-16). For the last part of the seating process it is useful, although not absolutely essential, to have a wooden needle (FIG. 17-17). A piece of wood that can be used edgewise to push the material along a rail or to open a hole is another tool with occasional uses (FIG. 17-18). A hammer, pincers, knife, and scissors are the only other tools needed.

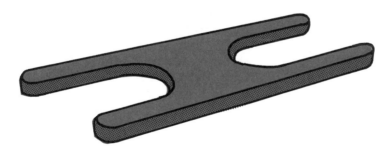

Fig. 17-16. A wooden shuttle.

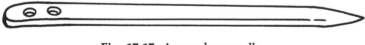

Fig. 17-17. A wooden needle.

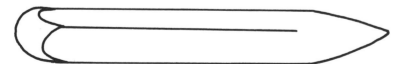

Fig. 17-18. You can use a piece of wood with a point to force the line
into the crevices or along rails.

The first step in creating the rush pattern on a chair frame is to nail the knotted end of the line (of rush, rope, or similar material) to a rail (FIG. 17-19). Then take the line over a rail near a leg, under it, and up through the center of the frame to the other rail. From this corner, take the line to the next corner, and repeat the process (FIG. 17-20). A repetition of this action completes a seat.

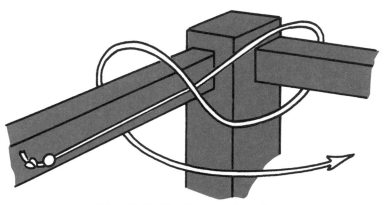

Fig. 17-19. Starting a rush pattern.

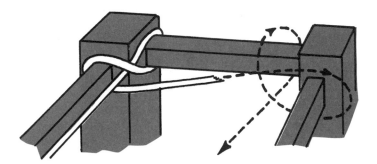

Fig. 17-20. Repeat the wrapping at the other three corners.

A good tension should be kept on the line at all times. This means holding the line against the wood whenever it crosses, until the next turns have been made. It is helpful if two people can position themselves at opposite sides so one can maintain tension while the other puts on the next turns.

As the work progresses, you will see the pattern build up from the corners, and the lengths of line between the corners will disappear inside. The pattern on the underside will be the same as that on the top. After a few times around the seat, check the squareness of the corner patterns. The pattern should be close-knit, with no bare wood showing between. It should be square to the corner. In a rectangular stool, you can use a straightedge to check. Any discrepancies are likely to be obvious to the eye without testing, however. Use the edge of a piece of wood to push the line wrapped around the rails to keep the angles true (FIG. 17-21). Check for squareness after every two or three rounds.

Twist in rushes as needed, but stagger the lengths of the separate strands so joints come at different places along the line. With seagrass or rope, make connecting knots between corners so the knot will be hidden (FIG. 17-22). If knots are needed in rushes, put them in the same place.

With a rectangular stool, you will reach a point where no more turns can be put on the short sides. Force in as many as you can by squeezing strands along the rails. If this step is not done, there is a tendency for gaps to show after some use. Continue working across the other way by an over-and-under figure-eight action (FIG. 17-22).

Another problem comes with a chair that is wider at the front than the back. If turns of line are continued in the ordinary way, the back would fill before the front. To correct for this problem, make occasional early turns twice

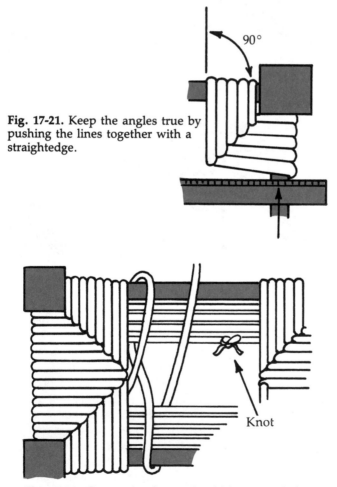

Fig. 17-21. Keep the angles true by pushing the lines together with a straightedge.

Fig. 17-22. Connecting knots should be concealed.

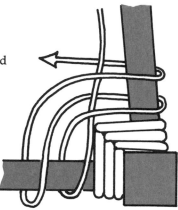

Fig. 17-23. Take double turns around the front legs to keep the pattern square.

around each of the front legs (FIG. 17-23). It is better to do this after every two or three complete rounds in the early stages than to wait until the bulk of the seat has been done. Use enough of these occasional twice-round turns at the front until the remaining gap at the front is about the same as that at the back rail.

Making rush patterns gets harder toward the end of the process. You must use a pointed stick to force open the center to pass more line. Use a wooden needle for the last few passes. Get as many turns around the rails as they will take. You can use the edge of a steel rule to push the line along and get in another turn. Using the maximum number of turns helps reduce the risk of a hole showing at the center of the pattern.

Finally, tack the line to the underside of a rail, cut off excess line, and push a few inches of it into the seat from below. The finished seat will be quite taut and might not seem very comfortable at first, but as the material settles down and the slight natural stretch takes place, there will be sufficient flexibility for comfort.

As you work the pattern, the hollow interior between top and bottom will become obvious. With manufactured seagrass or rope, there is no need to do anything about this space. With some types of rush, it might be advisable to fill the interior. When the rush pattern has been half done and the spaces are very apparent, you can push in waste rush, followed by more as the pattern progresses. This padding gives body to the seat and prevents the rushes from loosening excessively under pressure.

CHAIR CANING

Cane-seated chairs were in use in France and were introduced to England during the reign of Charles I, but they did not become popular until Charles II came to the throne. The method of caning has changed little since then and the seats of much modern and antique furniture will be found to have been worked in the same way. Similar caning is found on bedsteads and the sides of antique tables.

Several methods of weaving cane have been used, including a very close weave that was taken over the sides of the chair to give a covering almost like upholstery. Attempting to repeat this sort of covering is not advised. More common is an open pattern that makes use of holes drilled in the framework. Other methods have been devised that reduced some of the tedium of threading through holes, and it is possible to buy woven cane, already arranged as a patterned sheet, to fix as a panel.

Most chair cane grows in hot, swampy places, and is imported from Java and Sarawak. It trails and can grow to hundreds of feet in length. It has hooked thorns, which grip other vegetation. It is harvested into quite long pieces, which are then split and prepared for use. There are plastic substitutes, but obviously they would be inappropriate on a period piece of furniture.

Interweaving cane to make a seat can be done in many ways, and even in the more common patterns there are minor variations. If a damaged cane seat has to be stripped, or the repair is to a chair or stool that forms part of a set, examine the detail work before you remove old cane. You can cut away and discard old cane. Clean out all holes in the framework. At this stage the woodwork will almost certainly benefit from cleaning and probably repolishing.

Chair cane is supplied in bundles. Width is indicated by numbers. You can use pieces of the old cane as patterns when buying new cane. As supplied, the cane might be rather hard and brittle, but you can make it supple by soaking in cold water for a few minutes. It should be used damp, but not soaking wet. Plastic cane does not require soaking. You will have to accept the natural cane in whatever lengths it comes, but since 8 feet or so is about as much as can conveniently be worked at one time, this does not matter. Plastic cane is available supplied in a continuous length.

Essential tools are few: a good knife, and pegs. A pointed awl, called a *doubler*, can be used (FIG. 17-24). A similar tool with a long shaft and flat end is useful for cleaning holes (FIG. 17-25). Instead of the doubler, you can use a piece of waste wood pointed with a chisel or knife. You also can use pointed pieces of wood for temporary or permanent pegging. For permanent pegging, push in and snap off the pointed end, then cut a new point for the next time. You can use a larger wood or steel spike for opening spaces between canes. A *bodkin*, or spike with a hole in its end (FIG. 17-26) is used to pull strands through close weaving. A longer weaver (FIG. 17-27) performs a similar function across a seat.

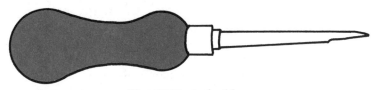

Fig. 17-24. A doubler.

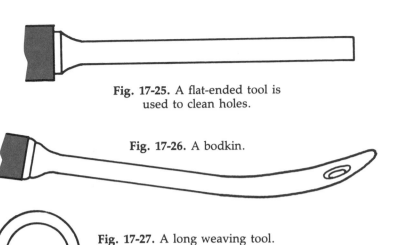

Fig. 17-25. A flat-ended tool is used to clean holes.

Fig. 17-26. A bodkin.

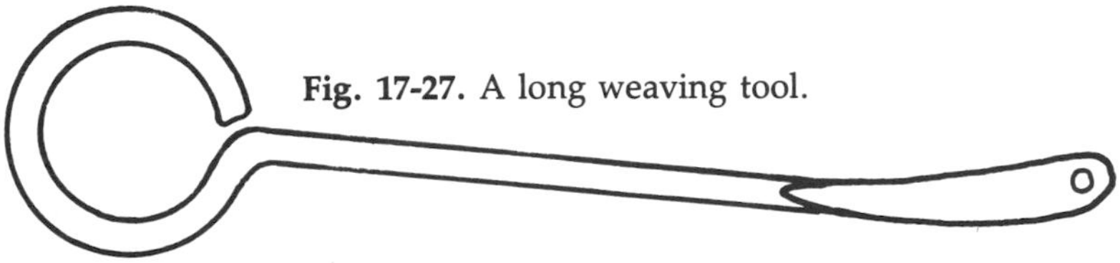

Fig. 17-27. A long weaving tool.

The holes in the chair frame need to be without obstruction. They should be bigger than the size of the cane. Cane makes a pattern in a single thickness. Thread it down through one hole, underneath, and up the next hole (FIG. 17-28). Avoid twisting the cane, and keep the glossary side uppermost all the time on the exposed parts.

It is possible to start a new length of cane by pegging old and new ends in holes, but it is safer to knot. Thread the end of the old piece up through a hole, making a loop underneath. Push the new end down through this hole and half-hitch it around the loop (FIG. 17-29). Pull the knot tight and continue working with the new piece. You can trim waste ends later.

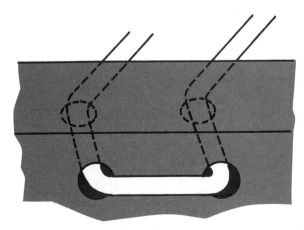

Fig. 17-28. Thread cane through one hole then through an adjacent hole.

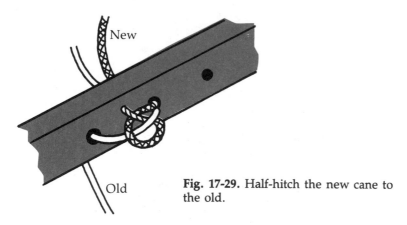

Fig. 17-29. Half-hitch the new cane to the old.

Cane Patterns

Most cane patterns have strands directly across the top at right angles to each other, with more strands woven diagonally. Variations come in the number of strands and how the overlaps are arranged. There are two basic patterns: *single-setting*, with only one strand between opposing holes in the first weaving, and *double-setting*, with two strands between opposing holes.

Double-setting, of course, is a little harder to do than single-setting. Use a single strand. Thread it through a hole near a corner with about 3 inches sticking out below and secure it with a peg. Pull the strand across the frame to the opposite hole. Thread it down this hole and up the next. Repeat the process, but do not thread through the corner holes. Put on a good tension each time and use a temporary peg to hold the tension at each hole while you work the cane to the next stage. This process puts strands of cane across one way (FIG. 17-30). Do the same in the other direction, with the strands on

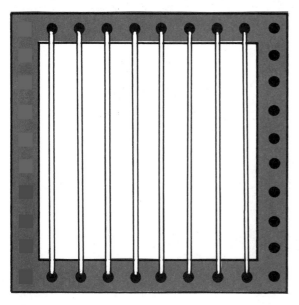

Fig. 17-30. The first step in double-setting.

top of the first (FIG. 17-31). Now thread strands in the opposite direction, using the same holes as were used initially. This time, however, pull the strands over the second group of strands (FIG. 17-32). Next, pull a fourth group of strands across the frame in the same direction as the very first strands, weaving over and under the second and third group of strands (FIG. 17-33). You can do this procedure by hand, but it is quicker to use a bodkin.

For a single-setting pattern, use only one strand of stouter cane, instead of the pairs of strands each way. From this point onward weaving is very similar. In both methods, maintain tension on the strands by pegs as the work progresses.

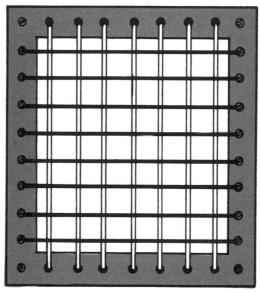

Fig. 17-31. Thread the second group of strands perpendicular to the first.

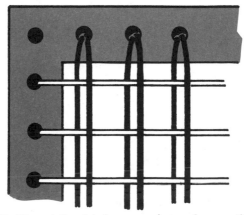

Fig. 17-32. Thread the third group of strands over the second. The second and third groups are parallel to each other.

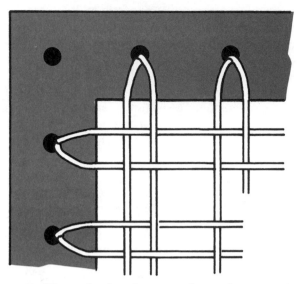

Fig. 17-33. Weave the fourth group of strands over and under the second and third.

In the double-setting method, push the crossing patterns close together so there is no doubt which are the spaces to be used for diagonal weaving. In double-setting, treat pairs of strands as single strands when doing diagonal weaves.

To weave diagonally on a double-setting pattern, start at a corner hole and go across to the opposite corner, over and under all the way (FIG. 17-34). Do this again between the same holes, but start under if the previous tucking started over, or vice versa. Do this between the other holes, paralleling the first diagonal weave.

Weave the other opposing diagonals in the same way, starting with two strands corner to corner and continuing until all holes are linked (FIG. 17-35).

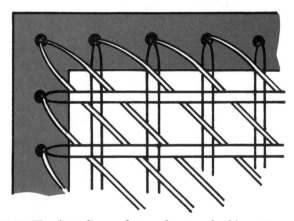

Fig. 17-34. The first diagonal strands on a double-setting pattern.

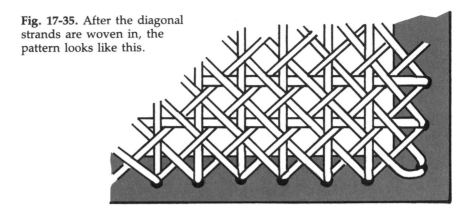

Fig. 17-35. After the diagonal strands are woven in, the pattern looks like this.

The pattern will get very tight and you will need a bodkin near the corner, if not also in the body of the seat.

Although this completes the pattern, the holes in the frame are exposed, and this would have an untidy appearance if left. The final step is covering the holes with a strand of cane, called *beading cane*, which may be wider than that used for weaving the pattern. It is held in place by thinner cane through the holes. Use a single length of the beading cane along one side, then another piece on the next side. Do not bend it around a corner.

First, point the end of the beading cane and push this end down a corner hole. Bend it and lay it over the holes along one side. Bring the thin cane up a hole, over the beading, and down the same hole to go underneath to the next hole, where you will repeat the action (FIG. 17-36). Do this all the way along the side, with a good tension. Then point the end of the beading cane and thrust it down the next corner hole. Repeat on the other sides. If any ends must be secured, use pegs and conceal them by the beading. To secure the ends of diagonals, twist them around any convenient loops underneath. Cut off stray ends flush.

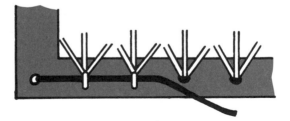

Fig. 17-36. Starting the beading cane.

Caning Other Shapes

Complications come when seats are not square or true rectangles. It is usual to make the woven pattern squared, rather than try to conform to the frame shape. Traditional chairs are often wider at the front than the back. The original arrangement will almost certainly have allowed for a square pattern.

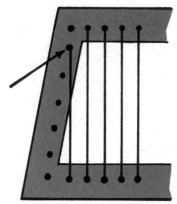

Fig. 17-37. Threading cane strands between side holes.

Start by caning between holes at back and front. Work outward. When all the rear holes, except the corners, have been used up, keep the canes parallel, but go to the side holes (FIG. 17-37).

Covering a round seat with cane is similar to covering a square seat, but holes around the curved perimeter must be taken up where they are convenient to make the pattern. This means not every hole is used every time, but tucking through holes is arranged as needed to keep pattern lines parallel.

With a circular or elliptical seat, count the holes and divide by four so as to obtain four points, which can be regarded as centers of four sides of the pattern. Work from the center outward and keep the canes parallel. Farther around the curve, you might need to miss some holes to retain parallel lines.

Arrange the diagonals so they will cross the first strands at 45 degrees. With a circular seat, this means starting at the holes halfway between those used to start the setting canes, but with any other sort of curve, you will need to judge the positions that will give the correct angles.

These instructions cover what is probably the best known pattern, but there are many variations. The diagonals might be put on first and the parallel canes put on singly or in pairs in a variety of patterns through them. Different sizes of cane might be mixed to give a different appearance. In all cases, the basic technique and tool work is the same as described, but you will need to follow the different patterns.

Section III
REFINISHING
OLD FURNITURE

18

Making Minor Surface Repairs

DO-IT-YOURSELF should use some caution before starting on the restoration of furniture. Planning is essential. This is important with modern furniture, as well as antique furniture. With antique furniture, however, a mistake in refinishing could mean disaster. The more valuable the piece, the more important it is to get an expert opinion.

HISTORY OF FURNITURE

Older furniture is classified according to its period or according to who designed or made it (SEE TABLE 18-1). Genuine examples from earliest days are unlikely to come the way of an amateur refinisher. There are many reproductions around, and there are a great many later examples of antique furniture that might require attention.

Until about 200 years ago the design and quality of British and American furniture lagged behind that of some European countries, particularly the Netherlands. Most items surviving from those days are chests. Oak was by far the most used wood. During the Cromwellian period, the manufacture of fine furniture was discouraged. After that, cabinetmaking began to make progress. There was an upsurge in the use of walnut and imported woods, which allowed the making of more delicate furniture with designs inappropriate to oak.

This upsurge continued with increasing refinement into the Queen Anne period. During the reigns of the Georges, there was a great increase in the quality and design of British furniture, which found its way into the American colonies.

Table 18-1. Antique Dates, Periods, and Styles

Tudor period	Henry VIII	1509 to 1547
	Edward VI	1547 to 1553
	Mary	1553 to 1558
Elizabethan period	Elizabeth	1558 to 1603
Jacobean period	James I	1603 to 1623
	Charles I	1625 to 1649
Cromwellian period	Cromwell	1649 to 1660
Carolean period	Charles II	1660 to 1685
	James II	1685 to 1688
Queen Anne period	William and Mary	1689 to 1702
	Queen Anne	1702 to 1714
	George I	1714 to 1724
Georgian period	George II	1724 to 1760
	George III	1760 to 1820
	George IV	1820 to 1830
Victorian period	William IV	1830 to 1837
	Queen Victoria	1837 to 1901

Names given to styles:

Chippendale I		
	1720 to 1779	Production from about 1750.
Chippendale II		
Chippendale III	1779 to 1805	Very little furniture output.
Brothers Adam	1728 to 1792	Designers of furniture made by others.
Hepplewhite	1760 to 1800	Firm carried on after death of Hepplewhite in 1786.
Sheraton	1751 to 1806	Designer, but some furniture made by him.
English Empire	1802 to 1840	Often copies of French pieces; in vogue until Victorian period.

All of the great designers and makers of this time put their designs into books, and these pattern books were used by other craftsmen, in addition to those employed by the famous cabinetmakers. At their peak, the Chippendales employed 20 to 30 cabinetmakers, but the large amount of Chippendale furniture available could only have been produced by the efforts of many other craftsmen as well.

Of course, many colonists brought furniture from England and other countries, so many original pieces from these days are in existence. It was not long, however, before American craftsmen were using the pattern books of Chippendale, Hepplewhite, and Sheraton as guides for making furniture with local woods, both for modest homes as well as large houses.

An example is the Windsor chair. It is said that George I, when hunting near Windsor, England, went into a farmhouse for a rest and liked his chair so much he had some made for use in Windsor Castle. By 1725, the design had reached America and was being made here. The English Windsor chair is made of beech, elm, and yew. It is still being made. American Windsor chairs had pine seats, local hardwood legs, and bent parts. Before long, the Windsor chair from Massachusetts had developed distinct differences from that of Virginia and other states.

By the end of the eighteenth century, furniture of a high standard was being made in America. Most pieces made before then are probably imported.

Of course, not all colonists were from England, and immigrants from elsewhere brought furniture or ideas from their own countries. So American furniture of a century or more ago had characteristics derived from this mixed background. The expert might be able to recognize these influences of what was becoming a distinctive American style.

GLUES AND FINISHES

Some idea of the history and age of a piece of furniture will provide a guide to its construction and the methods and materials to be used in preparing and refinishing it.

Any furniture made before World War II was almost certainly built with animal or fish glue, which have very little resistance to moisture. Even casein glue soon breaks down in damp conditions. Therefore, do not use too much water when cleaning this furniture. Do not soak the furniture. You can apply water with a cloth or brush and remove it before it has a chance to soak into joints and weaken them. Plywood of that age was also made with these glues. If water soaks in, the glue will part and the veneers will pucker. If you need to hose down any furniture to remove a violent chemical used in stripping or another process, do the job quickly. Doing it outside on a hot day, so moisture soon evaporates, is a good plan.

If you have used contact cement on modern veneers for fixing Formica tops, be careful with lacquer thinners because they will dissolve this cement.

The oldest furniture almost certainly will have an oil or wax finish. Some old furniture, particularly Victorian, might be French-polished. After World War I, however, sprayed lacquer came in. This is now the most common finish.

The approximate age of a piece of furniture tells you what finish to expect. This is important if you want to touch up or need to finish a new part to match old parts. It is also important if you want to strip the finish and start again because solvents differ in their effects. Alcohol, which softens French polish, might have little effect on oil.

With an opaque finish, brush marks will indicate paint, rather than lacquer, which is usually sprayed. The constitution of paint has changed over the years. The natural oils, resins, and other ingredients used up to the 1950s have given way to very different things. The solvents for old paint might have little effect on modern paints. The solvents needed for lacquer might be different again.

Clear brushed finishes are likely to be shellac or varnish. Even when a brushed finish has been there a long time and repeatedly polished, it is usually possible to look across the surface toward a light and distinguish brush marks. Spraying has a different appearance.

Shellac and varnish are very different things. Don't assume that you can always treat them alike. Also, although modern and traditional varnish might look alike on the wood, their chemical constitutions are very different.

If the old furniture is dirty and thick with polish and you are unable to identify the finish through it, clean a part of the surface with domestic detergent and water. Another mixture that will remove dirt and old polishing wax without much risk to the original finish is a mixture of denatured alcohol, vinegar, and kerosene in equal proportions. This will soften and remove most dirt, grease, and stain.

After a little experience, most people are able to distinguish one existing finish from another. The age of the piece will show what original finish was probably applied. Remember, however, that the original finish might not be the one on the wood now.

Refinishing seldom means stripping away the original finish and replacing it with a better one. The original finish might have been removed and replaced years ago. Refinishing usually entails stripping away the existing finishing and applying one that resembles the original.

An antique will have acquired a patina of age. There is no instant finish that will reproduce this if it is stripped off. It probably would be better to keep as much of the existing finish as possible and concentrate on repairing and touching up where necessary.

If the finish must come off, there are two principal ways of doing this: mechanically and chemically. Chemical stripping is probably the only method for a large or intricate piece of furniture where there is no doubt that the only way to make a good job of it is to work up from the bare wood. Mechanical stripping is done by scraping and sanding. It is usually more laborious, but if it is possible to revive the appearance without completely getting down to completely bare wood, this method might mean less total work in finally reaching the desired finish. Chemical stripping is messy, but effective. If your only work area is unsuitable for this, you might need to settle for mechanical stripping.

It is sometimes possible to refinish only part of the furniture. You need to be certain of the previous finish so you can use the same type again. The difficulty is in matching exactly. Even when you have the same materials, the new ones might not be able to duplicate the look of an aged finish. It is never advisable to join new and old finishes along a surface. Even if there has been new wood spliced on, it is better to clean off the old part down to bare wood. If the new finish goes up to the angle of a joint, a slight difference in appearance will usually be less obvious than if an attempt is made to blend new and old finishes along a rail or arm.

Minor surface repairs sometimes must precede a refinishing of damaged surfaces, and these techniques can mean the difference between a complete restoration and a discarded piece of furniture. Sometimes it's even possible to avoid refinishing altogether: a few repairs to an old finish can bring it back to life.

CLEANING

Dirt is not essential to antique furniture, as some people assume. It is merely a sign of neglect and should be removed. It might be difficult to identify the finish through layers of dirty polish. So the first step in doing minor repairs is to clean the surface to reach the finish.

You can try any household detergent, but use it with cold or lukewarm water, never hot water. Remove surplus detergent with clean water, otherwise it might affect the finishing materials that follow. The surface must be really dry before anything else is applied. Nearly all finishing materials are based on oil of some sort and oil does not mix with water, so the application of oil-based finishes over a damp base will result in poor adhesion and a surface that might blister or crack and come away.

In addition to detergent, you can use a mixture of equal parts of denatured alcohol, vinegar, and kerosene. Vinegar and water also might work. You can add kerosene or alcohol to soap and water. A warm mixture of water, turpentine, and linseed oil (in the proportions of 1 tablespoon of turpentine, 3 tablespoons of oil, and 1 quart of water) is another alternative. Any of these mixtures has the capacity to get through dirt, dissolve wax, and loosen other things that are marring the surface without much risk of damaging the applied finish beneath. More powerful solvents and cleaners might dissolve or soften the finish, as well as remove what has accumulated above it.

If the dirt resists all these mixtures, you might need to introduce friction. If the dirt or other foreign material is only on the surface, you can use steel wool with an oil or one of the cleaning mixtures. Thin machine oil is suitable. You can also use pumice powder on a cloth moistened with oil, instead of steel wool. In any case, wipe off frequently and inspect progress so you do not go too far.

To get at dirt in carvings, the recesses of moldings, or other intricate parts, use a brush such as an old toothbrush or shaving brush to apply the cleaner. For stubborn dirt, you might need something with stiffer bristles, such as a nail brush.

WHITE RINGS AND SPOTS

Hot or wet beverage containers stood on a surface might cause rings, which dry out as white marks. If the marks are not very bad or deep, they might disappear with one of the modern furniture polishes containing a cleaner. If a polish is not effective, you must remove it before trying another treatment.

Metal polish is effective on some marks. Use liquid metal polish and rub it over the surface gently. Cold cigarette ashes, dry or with a little water, rubbed over the marks also might be effective. With both methods, follow with wax polishing.

Flicking a cloth containing ammonia over the mark might work, particularly on lacquer. Do not rub with the cloth. It is the fumes that do the work. On some finishes, it might help to lightly wipe over with a cloth soaked in alcohol. If it is a brushed-shellac or French-polished surface, the use of alcohol might cause some existing finish to flow over the damage to hide it. On mahogany, wiping with linseed oil followed by rubbing with half a Brazil nut might hide the blemish.

BURNS

Hot liquids cause white rings, but flames or cigarettes might actually burn the finish and go through it to char the wood below. Of course, charred wood has completely lost its characteristics and there is no way to revive it. You might need to inlay another piece of wood or strip and level the surface. If the burn is only in the finish or isn't too deep, you might be able to deal with it as a local minor repair.

Scrape out the charred dust with a curved knife blade. Wet the hollow with paint thinner to show any burned dust remaining. Remove all the dust to expose sound wood or finish.

There are several ways of filling the hollow. You can use artist's oil paints, mixed to match the surrounding wood. Do not dilute. Smudge it into the hollow a little at a time. Wipe away surplus and leave it to harden. Spray it with lacquer or brush on another clear finish. Sand or use fine steel wool and apply more finish. Sight across the surface to see that it is level. When the repair has been leveled to your satisfaction, go over the whole surface with wax or other furniture polish.

There are other ways of filling the hollow. You can color beeswax and press it in while warm. You also can use colored shellac sticks. Melt the appropriate color, press it in the hollow, level it, then polish. Wax crayons also have possibilities. You can melt them in a spoon over a flame and mix them to get the right color. If you use a stove, there is less risk of soot getting into the wax. This wax is not as hard as wood, so after leveling, protect it with shellac, varnish, or lacquer.

SCRATCHES

You can deal with minor scratches by regular polishing. Most furniture polishes will clean out dirt from little scratches, and they have enough body to fill the scratches and make them less apparent.

Dirt trapped in a larger scratch might look even darker if polished over, so remove the dirt with one of the cleaning mixtures or by poking it out with a pointed tool.

Shallow scratches can sometimes have their edges run together without introducing any new material, but this depends on the finish. If you moisten a shellac finish with alcohol along the scratch and let it sit for some time—say two days—the softened edges might close. Rub over the surface with a cloth containing fine pumice and oil. When you polish it, the scratch should be gone.

A minor scratch on a varnished surface can sometimes be closed up with turpentine. Thinners might work on lacquer, but if the equipment is available, a respray is the best coverup.

For very large scratches, you can use Plastic Wood. It is unsuitable for fine cracks. Its color should match the surrounding finish, but if this cannot be arranged, it is possible to stain it. Plastic Wood will take the same finish as the surrounding wood.

You can melt shellac sticks into large recesses of all kinds. These colored sticks are used like sealing wax with a hot knife blade. A shellac stick is sometimes called a *beaumontage*, although this is the name of a traditional mixture used for filling holes.

BLACK RINGS AND SPOTS

Black spots are not as easy to remove as white spots. The black is a result of long wetting, so the black tint must be bleached out. Domestic bleach might work, or you can brush on a concentrated solution of oxalic acid. This solution works almost instantaneously, so be ready to wipe it off with a damp cloth. A concentrated solution can be made with about 3 tablespoons of oxalic acid crystals and 1 cup of hot water. Pour the crystals in the hot water while stirring. Stir until all the crystals are dissolved.

WARNING

Oxalic acid is very poisonous so take care in its use, storage, and disposal.

This bleaching is unlikely to have much effect on the existing finish, so after you deal with the black mark, you can bleach ink or other dark liquids that have penetrated the finish in the same way.

HAZE

After a long time, the atmosphere will affect most finishes. There might be a grayish or whitish haze to the finish, which is sometimes only apparent when viewed from particular angles. This effect is only on the thinnest surface layer of the finish.

To get rid of this effect, you must remove the outer film of the finish. Clean off dirt and polish to completely expose the finish. Go over the surface with the finest steel wool, working with the grain as much as possible. The dulling effect of this process will obscure the haze. To check if you have rubbed far enough, moisten the surface with turpentine. If you can still see the haze, rub more but do not wear the finish away unnecessarily. Wipe the dust away, preferably with a tack rag. Go over the surface with wax or liquid furniture polish.

CRACKED FINISH

An old finish might become covered with a mass of small cracks as a result of age or expansion and contraction of the wood underneath. It does not happen with wax or oil finishes, which remain sufficiently elastic, but some lacquer and shellac finishes might eventually become hard and brittle so any movement of the base will crack them. You might need to strip them and start again, but there are ways of running the cracks together again.

If it is a lacquer surface, go over it with lacquer thinner. Work in a ventilated but dry and warm place. Any humidity might cause clouding of the finish. Work quickly all over the surface. The whole surface should become a paintlike consistency. Lightly brush it smooth, then let it dry completely. Go over it with steel wool and finish with a furniture polish.

Deal with shellac surfaces in the same way as lacquer surfaces, but use alcohol diluted with about 10 percent lacquer thinner.

19

Furniture Stripping

IF THE FINISH on a piece of furniture is not worth being revived, the only hope for the furniture, if it is structurally sound, is to strip the finish and start again from the bare wood. This can be a very satisfying activity and can result in a wreck being brought back into use. Something that was properly designed and constructed might justify a considerable amount of work in removing the old finish and applying a new one. There could be a surprising increase in value, possibly from negligible or no value to antique status.

The early stages might be very messy, and most people would not regard the work as pleasant. The chemicals needed to remove some finishes must be handled carefully because they can be dangerous, both to the user and to items in the vicinity. Something that will dissolve a finish also might ruin clothing, eat into upholstery, and do other damage if allowed to go where it should not. If you use chemical strippers, apply them outdoors in a place where you can use plenty of water.

The first thing to do with an article that is to be stripped is to clean it. Although chemical strippers often will attack a finish rapidly, they might not attack the dirt on top of it. Remove dirt with water and detergent, which will not affect any wax on the surface. Wiping with a cloth soaked in turpentine should remove wax. If the surface still seems dirty after this treatment, use detergent and water again. Much old furniture was joined with glues that are not waterproof, so use a minimum amount of water and wipe it off after cleaning each part. Do not soak the furniture when washing it.

You need to know what the existing finish is. Paint is fairly obvious, but there might be doubt about a clear finish. Even an opaque finish that looks like paint might be lacquer. Use an inconspicuous part for testing and rub with turpentine. If the surface softens and begins to dissolve, it is paint or varnish. Try using alcohol. If the surface is shellac, it will soon soften. If it is a lacquer finish, only lacquer thinner will have any effect on it.

If the furniture has knobs, hinges, handles, or other metal or plastic parts that can be removed, take them off. If the furniture will come apart in any way, separate all you can and deal with parts individually. Drawers should come out. Taking off hinges might release doors and allow shelves to be withdrawn. Some tables have tops made up of moving leaves that can be released. Even some tables with apparently fixed tops have screws below that will allow the top to come off.

DRY STRIPPING

Although most stripping is done with liquids and pastes, it is sometimes possible to get down to the bare wood by mechanical means. This is called *dry stripping*. If the piece of furniture was discarded by someone and left outside, it is likely that much of the finish has peeled away. Mechanical methods can then remove what is left and, at the same time, do something to improve the surface in readiness for the new finish.

Usually, mechanical stripping is more appropriate to small items. The mess associated with liquids and pastes might not be justified then, but for large items with the finish still firmly attached, they would be more efficient and less trouble.

Stripping can be done with a hand scraper, either the cabinet type or the hook type that can be pulled. The edge of a piece of broken glass will also make an effective scraper. Use enough pressure to get the cutting edge of the scraper through most of the finish. Experiment with the angle that gets the best cut. Holding the scraper so it travels with a slicing action might be more effective than a straight pull or push.

Hand sanding is possible, but can be rather slow. Use a coarse abrasive paper at first. Many finishes produce a dust that quickly clogs fine paper. Use the paper wrapped around a block and work with the grain in case any grit scratches right through to the wood. These marks would show if made across the grain. When bare wood is within sight, change to a finer abrasive.

A belt or orbital sander will be quicker than hand sanding. Start with a coarse grit, say No. 80, because of the risk of clogging, and change to a finer grade as you reach bare wood.

Sanding and scraping might become tedious and unsatisfactory on intricate moldings and other places where there is not much flat or broadly curved areas. Even on small work, it is then probably wiser to use a chemical stripper.

WET STRIPPING

There are a great many chemical strippers. Some are simple solvents, but those needed for paint and varnish are chemical mixtures. They are available in prepared form, and for occasional use this is the best way of getting them. If you need to do much stripping, the trouble of mixing your own stripper might be justified. The various constituents bought in bulk should be cheaper, but some of them need careful handling and storage.

Take certain precautions when using chemical strippers. It is usually best to work outdoors. If you do work in an enclosed place, see that there is adequate ventilation so any fumes given off are dispersed rapidly. Otherwise, some of them might harm your eyes, throat, or skin. Ventilation is also important because many of the fumes are combustible: they might ignite spontaneously if allowed to concentrate. Obviously, you should not smoke or have an open flame anywhere near the work area.

Old clothes and a rubber apron are advisable. Cover your arms, and wear eye goggles and strong rubber gloves. You also might wish to use a barrier cream on your skin.

If possible, work on a concrete surface and have a hose available that can wash the surplus stripper and its resultant gunk away. You also need a few buckets to collect the mess that is scraped off. If you must work inside, cover the floor with paper, plastic, cloth, or other things. Many chemical strippers will attack these coverings, however, so be prepared to gather them up and dispose of them. If a hose isn't handy to wash away residue, you will need plenty of water to apply with brush and sponge.

Don't work around children or animals. Store the strippers in a secure place. Do not leave any of the liquids in open containers; they can evaporate quickly.

Chemical strippers are rather harsh on anything they touch, so you must be prepared to discard things. You can use cloth pads and fine steel wool, which will function something like a sponge, as well as provide some abrasive qualities. Use old brushes; they will last a reasonable time. You need stiff-bristled brushes to get into crevices, and old tooth and nail brushes for carvings and moldings. For the grooves between parts of turned work, you can use string soaked in chemical stripper and pull it around. You can also break burlap or other coarse material into pieces to get chemical stripper into awkward places.

Remove the softened finish with a scraper. The best type has a broad blunt end (FIG. 19-1). It is not intended to cut, but merely lifts the gunk as it is pushed along. A sharper end might dig into the wood. You can use a wooden scraper (FIG. 19-2) or a putty knife—the type cut square across the end—in the same way. Scrapers can be quite crude, as long as they have thin edges to get under the paint or varnish that has softened.

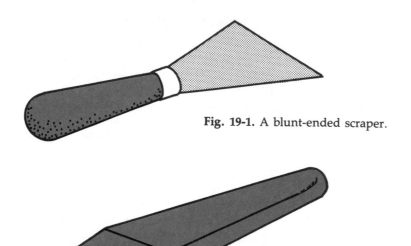

Fig. 19-1. A blunt-ended scraper.

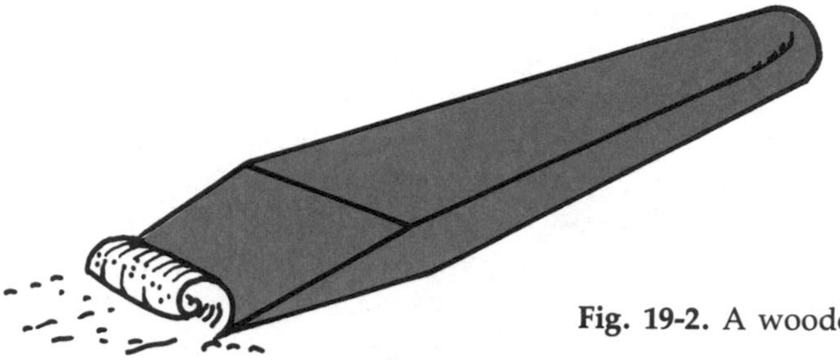

Fig. 19-2. A wooden scraper.

CHEMICAL STRIPPERS

You can remove lacquer with lacquer thinners or shellac mixed with alcohol. Both solvents evaporate quickly, so you must apply them lavishly, and remove the softened finish before the solvent in it has evaporated. This usually means working on only part of an area at a time, scraping almost immediately after putting on the solvent. If you have spray equipment, spray the solvent with one hand while the other hand scrapes.

It may be necessary to work on a part several times if there is much lacquer or shellac to be removed. You can also use paint stripper on shellac and some lacquers. If you strip a surface with alcohol or lacquer thinners, you can apply a new finish without neutralizing the surface.

Chemical strippers for paint and varnish are broadly divided into solvents and caustics. The solvent types are less harmful, but the recommended precautions should still be observed. Paint and varnish removers bought in a can are likely to be of the solvent type. Liquid removers are suitable for flat surfaces, but there are paste removers that contain starch or other stiffeners that helps them to resist sliding away on vertical or sloping surfaces.

A solvent paint remover contains wax. The wax forms a thin skin as the remover is applied and prevents the volatile liquids in the remover from evaporating too quickly. Therefore, do not brush or rub over the remover after you apply it. Flow it on generously and leave it. Working the brush or cloth backward and forward breaks the wax skin and makes it ineffective.

After using a stripper containing wax, go over the surface with a cloth soaked in alcohol. Rub hard with this and change the cloth surface frequently so you pull any residue of wax out of the pores of the wood. Also go over carvings and moldings with a brush and alcohol. This is an important step. Although wax is a good thing to put on top of a finish, if it is allowed to remain under a new finish, it will affect its adhesion.

Solvent paint and varnish removers contain a mixture of individual solvents. One remover that can be made consists of one part denatured alcohol, one part acetone, and one part benzol, to which has been added a small amount of paraffin wax shavings.

Of the caustic removers or strippers, a common one is lye (caustic soda). This is used with water and a little cornstarch. First, dissolve the cornstarch in cold water—1 cup of cornstarch to 2 cups of water is about right—and heat until the mixture thickens. Set this mixture aside. In a plastic bucket dissolve 12 ounces (3 or 4 tablespoons) of lye in 1 quart of cold water.

WARNING

Add the lye crystals to the water, not the water to the lye. Adding water to lye can cause boiling and spattering with danger to eyes, skin, and clothing. Remember to protect your eyes and wear rubber gloves. Have the cornstarch mixture in another plastic bucket and slowly mix in the lye solution. This mixture can be used warm or cold.

Apply the solution to the finish and let it work for about 10 minutes. Watch the reaction and add more if necessary. The paint or varnish should completely loosen so it can be pushed off with a scraper. A scrubbing brush or steel wool might help on stubborn parts.

Next, use water to wash the surface after stripping. If this is done thoroughly, you might not need to treat the surface in any other way, except drying, before you start to refinish.

Another caustic stripper is trisodium phosphate or TSP. A fairly concentrated solution is made in hot water (2 or 3 pounds of the powder in 1 gallon of water). Use it hot in a very similar way to lye, with several applications if necessary.

Caustic strippers must be used with great care. If you suspect the furniture of being vulnerable to water, there is a risk of damage to glued joints.

It is inadvisable to mix different strippers. Sometimes, however, you might not get much success with the first stripper you try. Do not go straight into using another stripper, but carry the first treatment through to its end, particularly washing off or neutralizing. However, it is safe to follow a commercial solvent paint remover with trisodium phosphate, using it to remove the remains of the first paint remover, as well as the reluctant paint.

After working with chemical strippers, dispose of cloths and other things that have been used with the solutions. Do not pack cloths soaked in solvent or chemical stripper into a bucket and leave them. Spontaneous combustion might result, as well as unpleasant or harmful fumes. Put the cloths in water and dispose of them away from the work area. Similarly, remove paper, plastic, and other materials that have become soiled.

Take the furniture away from the place where it was stripped. Put it where it can dry in a well-ventilated place. Although it is possible to apply the new finish soon after using some strippers, it is better to let the wood dry, particularly if you think you will need to do sanding and scraping to get a good surface for refinishing.

Clean the work area and put away any remaining chemicals. You have not finished stripping until you have removed all risk of danger.

20

Furniture Refinishing

WHEN ALL OF THE OLD FINISH has been stripped, the furniture is ready to receive its new finish. If the new finish is to be paint or opaque lacquer, any discoloration will not matter because it will be hidden. If the new finish is to be clear, even if there will be stain underneath, you will probably need to even the color in the wood before you begin new treatment.

PREPARATIONS

Stain and some of the previous finish almost certainly will be trapped in the pores of the wood. This might not matter, if the color is even. In fact, some collectors of restored antique furniture regard this as evidence of age and something that improves, rather than detracts from, the quality and value of the furniture. What has to be guarded against is uneven color and texture that will show through the new finish.

Some stains might be difficult to remove from the pores of the wood. Whether much stain comes away with stripping of the finish depends on the type of stain. A water stain might need a wipe with water to remove more stain or to even streakiness. Spirit stain might have responded to a solvent-type chemical stripper, but you can do any local clearing after stripping by wiping with alcohol. If the stain had an oil base, wiping is better done with benzene or naphtha. The type of stain might have become apparent during earlier treatment, since one of the chemical strippers used might have dissolved it. Otherwise, you might need to experiment to discover what to use for removing or evening the stain.

The aim, at this stage, is to get an even color. It might not be the natural color of the wood, but the general appearance should be uniform.

Getting an even color means darkening light parts, lightening dark parts, or both. Wiping with solvents might be all that is needed. Using a cloth pad soaked in solvent in all directions on a surface might break down the streakiness left from stripping. The solvent will lift some stain from dark parts and blend parts that show sudden changes from dark to light. Change the surface of the cloth pad frequently.

If a dark part must be lightened, use one of the bleaching techniques described in Section 1. Oxalic acid will probably be the most convenient. You can apply the bleach with a cloth over a broad area, or with a small brush over a small area.

In addition to uneven stain, there might be marks in old furniture from rusting screws or prolonged contact with metal parts. There might be marks from spilled ink or other liquid. Now is the time to attack these marks by careful application of bleach. Oak is particularly prone to staining from contact with steel. Brass is much less troublesome.

If you must darken a light part, use thin stain. Apply the stain and wipe off most of it. Continue this procedure until you have the color you want. Using a thick or dark stain the first time is risky. You could overdo it and need to bleach before making another attempt.

Pine and other softwoods can suffer from uneven coloring as they age. Some old softwood furniture was made from several woods, which could have aged to different colors. Even two parts of the same wood might be different. Sapwoods and heartwood are no different in appearance in most softwoods when newly worked, but sometimes the sapwood ages to a gray color alongside the unchanged heartwood. Fortunately, this grayness usually responds to bleach.

Much pioneer and colonial furniture was made of softwoods, and the treatment given varied according to available materials. Some stains and finishes were made from pigments and liquids available locally, but most should respond to strippers and further treatment as already described.

Knotty pine was not always regarded as attractive, and finishes were used to disguise the knots without completely hiding the grain. One of these finishes used a red pigment dissolved in skim milk. The color was like cherry or mahogany, although the pine grain was visible.

This is a stubborn finish to remove, and you must do a combination of mechanical and chemical stripping. Alcohol will soften the finish. While you keep the surface moistened with alcohol, rub it with steel wool or coarse abrasive paper, either by hand or with an electric sander. The red pigment has a considerable penetration into softwood, so even when the surface has been brought down to bare wood, there will be redness in the grain. This is attractive and can be preserved as evidence of age showing through the new finish.

Staining and bleaching usually must be used with sanding and scraping. It is unlikely that a stripped surface will be left in a fit state for the immediate application of paint, varnish, lacquer, or other finish. This grain might have been raised as a result of the use of liquids, and might respond to scraping or sanding. Detailed instructions for obtaining a good wood surface are given in Section 1. Follow them, but remember that sanding and scraping might affect coloring. Scraping takes away some of the surface—not as much as planing, but more than sanding. This reduction of surface can affect appearance, which might not matter if you scrape the whole thing. If you only scrape part of the surface and it adjoins a sanded part, there might be a slight difference in appearance after finishing, although the untreated wood looks the same.

If you are dealing with an antique, avoid too drastic a treatment of the surface. Do all the sanding necessary, but avoid the need to work down to a new surface, unless the old surface is so badly damaged that planing, scraping, or heavy sanding is needed. The old surface will have acquired a patina of age, which you should preserve if possible.

Don't get carried away when using a power sander on an open surface. In the more inaccessible parts, you will need to use a considerable amount of hand sanding. Moldings and carvings can be particularly troublesome, but if you are to achieve an even result, these need just as much cleaning and sanding. Be particularly careful of deep grooves and recesses. Get the residue of stripping and sanding out with a spike or pointed scraper. It is useful to have a vacuum cleaner and a tack rag to go over the furniture before starting on the new finish.

If you need to make any repairs, work them in with the surface preparatory work. If a joint is loose, it might be more convenient to sand while the pieces can be pulled apart. In general, do repairs before sanding, including filling in any dents or holes. Some stoppings tend to change color slightly after sanding. You will need to coordinate coloring, bleaching, and sanding, and you might need to do some trial and error to get a coloring result that is reasonably uniform in the finished piece of furniture.

As a final step before refinishing, look over the work toward a light. There should be a uniform flat mat appearance. A hint of a sheen anywhere could indicate a little of the old finish still remaining. It might not matter for an opaque finish, but with a clear finish it could affect the color or texture, showing a difference at that spot. A little more sanding over the particular area is probably all that is needed.

If you have done any new gluing, remove surplus from the surface. Use the minimum necessary in a joint. If there is an excess, however, it is not usually sufficient to just wipe it away. With most modern glues, this leaves glue blocking the wood pores around the joint and prevents an even penetration of stain or finish. It is better to let the glue almost harden and cut it away with a chisel, then lightly sand.

SELECTING A NEW FINISH

Before starting to build up a finish again after stripping and preparing the wood, spend some time deciding on what you are aiming at. If the piece of furniture is a genuine antique, it should be given a finish that is appropriate. When you have finished your work, the result should look as it might have a century ago. It might not, in fact, be finished in exactly the same way, but it will look like it. There is no reason why you should not take advantage of improvements in methods and materials, providing they achieve similar results to those originally employed. It would be inappropriate to spray a high-gloss lacquer on something that would only look right with a more mellow and subtle sheen of wax. There is nothing wrong, though, with using spray in the early stages of shellac finishing, if this would speed the eventual buildup of a suitable hand-polished surface.

Of course, if the furniture is not an antique and is a comparatively modern piece thrown out or discarded by someone else, you can do almost anything you like to it. Whatever you do should improve it. If it is made of softwood and plywood and has been neglected, it might only be suitable for an opaque finish, applied by brush or spray. If it is hardwood but has been left in the open, the many parts might have weathered or absorbed dirt. So despite your efforts at bleaching and cleaning, a natural finish would look uneven and unattractive. It might be better covered with paint or opaque lacquer. If you still want the grain to show through, a fairly dark stain might be the only way to disguise the differences in wood color.

Many furniture restorers try to keep the wood grain showing if possible. They prefer wood in its natural color. If that is impossible, they stain it and use a transparent finish, so all of the beauty of the texture and grain of the wood shows through. Only as a last resort would they cover the wood with an opaque finish. When you cannot see through the finish, the base material might be metal, plastic, or other material, instead of wood. Although those materials have their places in modern furniture, there is nothing like wood for the best furniture. So why destroy the evidence?

Of course, all these considerations must be tempered with a knowledge of where and how the restored piece is to be used. If it will be in a kitchen or laundry, a tough opaque finish is more appropriate than a natural one. If it is to go in a room where everything else is stained a dark color, a very light or natural finish might be inappropriate. If the only hope of getting an acceptable finish on a restored piece is to apply dark stain, and the place where it is to be used is stocked with light furniture, think about it. The furniture in a room does not need to be uniform in finish; something that contrasts with the other things can look right. Much depends on your sense of interior design.

If the furniture being restored can be regarded as an individual piece, without consideration of where it is to go, your choices are multiplied. If it is a rescued piece of no particular value and it is to be a present or for sale, you can finish it in any way you wish. It might provide an opportunity for experiment. Do not be too daring, however. Multicolored surfaces or a covering with fairy tale decals may be objectionable to friends and customers.

REFINISHING METHOD

The actual methods of refinishing are similar to those described for finishing new wood. You might also need to make some of the repairs described in Section 2. Only methods of dealing with wood that has already had one finish applied and removed are given here.

The difference between stripped wood and new wood is mainly that stripped wood will almost certainly have remnants of the earlier finish trapped in the pores of the grain. How much depends on what the original finish was and how thoroughly the stripping was done. It is almost impossible to completely remove particles of an earlier finish that have entered the pores. The solvents might get some out, but they also wash some farther in. This does not matter, but should be allowed for, particularly when staining.

Another difference might be in the quality of the wood. Seasoning is a long process. Despite the efficiency of modern methods of seasoning, wood needs time to achieve the stable condition that results from thorough seasoning. New wood might be in acceptable condition, with the correct degree of moisture content arrived at by modern scientific control. As it ages, however, cracks might develop or open, knots might loosen, or other flaws might slowly become apparent. The wood in an old piece of furniture should have passed this stage. The condition in which you find it after stripping is unlikely to change, and you can go ahead on the assumption that no problems resulting from the wood should arise after you have finished work on it. This is also one reason for keeping old wood in sound condition. If you break up a piece of furniture, wood rescued from it might be better for repairing another piece than new wood from the mill or wood yard.

Make sure the wood is absolutely dry. If you have had to moisten to raise grain before sanding, let all of the moisture evaporate. Wiping with a cloth soaked in alcohol will pull out water. If the chemical stripper has required neutralizing, make sure the neutralizer has evaporated. If there is no rush to refinish, allow the wood to dry for several days.

Use a vacuum cleaner and a tack rag on the wood immediately before you start to refinish. Go slowly over the surface with the end of the hose of the vacuum cleaner pointing straight at the wood to pull out any dust in the pores that is free enough to come away. Follow immediately with the first finishing stage to seal the wood before it can take up any more dust.

If the first treatment is stain, apply it thinly, preferably with a cloth. Use a water or oil stain. Spirit stain might dry too quickly. Spread the stain and wipe off surplus. In this way, you can watch variations in absorption. There will almost certainly be some variations as a result of varying amounts of residue in the pores of the wood. Continue to apply thin coats, allowing more stain on parts that need darkening. Building up to the required color in this way is more likely to result in an even appearance than applying one liberal coat of dark stain.

Variations in absorption might be a problem with whatever is applied next. You might need to use several layers to obtain an even finish. You can use shellac where it suits what is to follow. Rub down between coats as necessary to fill the grain and provide a smooth base for further finishing. Lacquer may be sprayed on and rubbed down in the same way.

Since the wood should have been filled under the old finish, it is unlikely that any very lavish treatment will be needed with paste or other filler. If there is doubt, test an inconspicuous part of the furniture with and without filler. If there are obviously open parts of the grain, you might want to use filler all over for an even finish. On antique oak, there might never have been any filler, so the hollows over the wider gaps in the grain may be accepted in the new finish as being appropriate to the particular furniture, even when the application of filler would have given a smooth, even sheen.

Varnish will make its own filler, unless the stripped wood is very absorbent. If you must apply too many coats merely to fill the grain, another filler would be quicker and more economical.

Consider the final effect you desire. A hard gloss is protective and easily cleaned, but too brilliant a sheen might not be appropriate to the piece of furniture. An antique might have its sprayed or brushed finish rubbed down and waxed, or be finished by French polishing.

For a painted finish, pay attention to the quality of the prepared surface, but do not worry if the wood color is uneven. Shellac makes a good, quick base for painting. Watch absorption and look across the dried surface to see where dullness indicates soaking in. Apply more where necessary and sand level. Once the surface has been sealed in this way, painting is no different than for new work, as described earlier.

21

Special Techniques

SPECIAL RESTORATION METHODS demand imagination. You can make furniture look old or individual or elegant or anything you wish. All you need is a knowledge of a few techniques and some good ideas.

AGE SIMULATION

New work and old furniture that's being restored can be made to look old. This is sometimes called *furniture faking*, which it would be if an attempt was made to pass off the furniture as a genuine antique. The look of antiquity is attractive, however, and there is certainly nothing wrong with trying to achieve such a look.

There are certain processes described as *antiquing* that would certainly not deceive anyone. Antiquing kits are available that will give a finish with some semblance of antiquity. Other treatments can be applied to old furniture to make it look older. If you like an antique appearance, there is no reason why you should not set out to make an apparent antique from new wood.

A knowledge of furniture antiquing is useful when you need to repair old furniture. If you must make a new part and build it into a genuine antique piece of furniture, it is obvious that you must make it match, in the appearance of both age and wear, using methods already described.

Try visualizing how the parts of a piece of furniture might wear over a century or so of use. Unless the piece has been kept almost in museum conditions, fair wear and tear will have taken their toll. A rail on which feet might have rested will have the squareness worn away. If it is a turned rail, there might have been enough foot wear to have hollowed a side of the turning. Similarly, table legs might have been knocked by a chair or other seat.

A tabletop used for meals might have slight hollows worn by the regular use of dishes on one spot. The exposed edge of the top of a table or cabinet is likely to have been knocked and worn, so there are irregularities in the appearance. These are all wear marks that can be simulated.

Simulating wear and damage is aptly described as *distressing*. With new wood, some of the distressing will need to be done before applying stain or finish, but it would be wrong to imitate all the damage and wear on the bare wood and then finish over it. Wear to the old work would have happened *after* the surfaces had been finished. Much of the finish would have been worn through. Almost certainly, however, polish or other treatment to revive the finish would have been applied at intervals over the bare, or near bare, wood as well as over the parts retaining their full finish. This must be taken into account. If heavy wear is to be assumed, as for a rail used as a footrest, you can do some shaping before you apply a finish, but you can simulate wearing away followed by more wax or other polish.

To accomplish shaping, wrap abrasive paper around a strip of wood and use it like a file. If the wood is given a curved cross section (FIG. 21-1), the resulting shaping will be more realistic. Rock the tool both in the length and sideways. The shaping must not appear too regular or obviously made much quicker than normal wear would have achieved. Definite cuts, as might result from the use of a chisel or knife, are not wanted. If you use such tools to shape something near the required depth, make sure there is plenty of sanding afterward that destroys tool marks and disguises any evenness of tool cuts.

In addition to wear in appropriate places, very old furniture will have suffered from dents. A dent compresses the wood fibers, instead of wearing them away. Dents are made by striking the wood, not by cutting or wearing away dents and hollows.

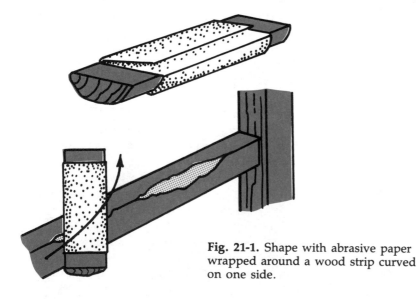

Fig. 21-1. Shape with abrasive paper wrapped around a wood strip curved on one side.

You can obtain the effect of dents over the years in several ways. You can gather a piece of chain into a ball and pound it on the surface by hand (FIG. 21-2). Another way is to use a piece of rock in the hand. Coral rock is favored. You can make direct hits with an iron rod, either with its side or end, depending on what sort of damage you want to simulate.

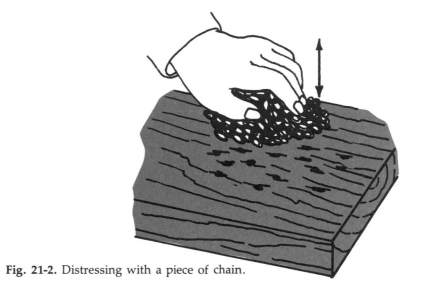

Fig. 21-2. Distressing with a piece of chain.

Whatever method you use, avoid uniformity. Damage from dents over the years would not follow a regular pattern, so make sure your pounding of the surface is random. Do not be overenthusiastic with your denting. Most furniture owners would have used reasonable precautions over the years, and it is unlikely they will have let the wood get excessively battered. Any marks will be a result of accidents that escaped their care. Try to make your simulated damage give this impression.

Quite often, dents cause a darkening of the wood, so you might need to use a thick stain on your applied dents. Staining must be kept local to the damage. Do not allow stain to soak along the grain and blend gradually into the wood.

Instead of one of the usual stains, use artist's oil color in turpentine. Vandyke brown, mixed fairly thickly, should give the right effect on most woods. You can use a small artist's brush to paint on the stain, but avoid uniformity. A better way of getting uneven stain marks is to cover the ball of chain with stain so it deposits stain at the same time it makes dents.

An old finish sometimes acquires small dark dots. You can simulate this random arrangement of small dots by splattering with a brush. Use a paint or varnish brush and a stick. Use the same thick stain as suggested for the dents. Experiment first on scrap wood or a piece of paper. Hold the stick in one hand and knock the ferrule or handle of the brush against it so stain is thrown on the surface (FIG. 21-3). Varying the amount of stain and the hitting

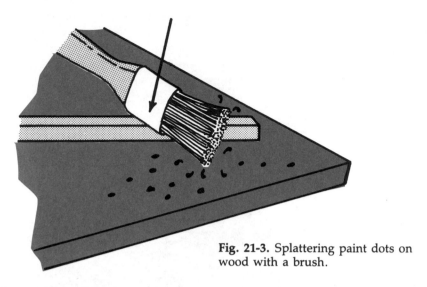

Fig. 21-3. Splattering paint dots on wood with a brush.

force will regulate the size and position of the dots. Only quite small dots are required. When practice splattering has produced a satisfactory result, work over the wood.

You can distress with dents and splatter dots before final finishing, but after some finish has been applied. For color treatment, shellac, lacquer, or varnish rubbed in makes a suitable base. If the surface of the wood is absorbent, there is a risk of the color spreading. When you apply color allow it to dry completely then protect it by further coats of finish.

Sometimes a very old finish acquires many fine dark lines, probably a result of cracking of the finish and the entry of dirt. This finish might have been polished over, but the dark lines remain. The effect is not from the grain of the wood, so the lines can be in any direction.

To distress wood with these lines, paint them on. Use artist's brushes. A fine one will do all the lines, but having more than one brush allows an easier application of lines of different sizes, as they would be in genuinely aged furniture. Draw fine lines with thick stain, as suggested for splattering and denting. Let the lines be random and mostly short (FIG. 21-4). Use very little stain in the brush at each application so the lines are irregular in outline.

After distressing wood, it spoils the effect to give a finish that could not have been used a century ago. Oil and wax are safe choices, while French polishing would be acceptable. Shellac or lacquer might be a quicker way of filling the grain and building up something on which to base the final finish, but it is what goes on top that is most important.

Whatever the original finish on an old piece of furniture, it is likely that the patina of age is the result of polishing at intervals over a very long time, usually with wax. In making a simulated antique, particularly if it is to be a repaired part of a genuine antique, you will need to use wax polish, furniture cream, and other things that are really finish revivers. For the best results, allow a few weeks, at least, between applications.

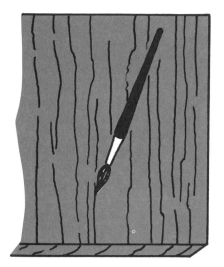

Fig. 21-4. Age lines can be painted on with a small brush.

ANTIQUING

You can mellow the surface of painted furniture by antiquing. This kind of antiquing involves the application of antique glaze. The glaze is usually darker than the surface it is to be applied to. It is rubbed on, then most of it is rubbed off. Irregularities, such as carvings and moldings are emphasized by the glaze. Angles and corners become more defined. Contrasts are emphasized. Light colors benefit from the treatment.

Suitable antique glazes are available alone or in complete kits. Alternatively, you can make a glaze by using the appropriate oil color with an equal amount of linseed oil, with a little turpentine. You can add a very small amount of dryer. In another mixture, mix the oil color with turpentine in about equal amounts, then add about half as much varnish. Do not mix more glaze than is needed for the work at hand, and try to get a creamlike consistency that can be brushed.

The choice of oil color must be related to the base color and the desired effect. To obtain a yellowish-brown, use burnt umber or raw sienna. This mixture is used when the base paint is a pastel or light shade; it can be used with white or any pale color, but it is unsuitable for the more pronounced colors, such as red and green. Umber also can be used over gold paint. Lampblack is used in the glaze over red, green, or other strong background colors, as well as on silver paint.

If the background paint has been newly applied, make sure it has dried completely. Otherwise the glaze will mix with it, causing a muddy result.

Brush on the glaze to cover the surface being treated. You can only do a portion of the surface at a time if it is a large object. The glaze will cover and obscure the original color. Work into any corners, grooves, and other irregularities. Wipe off unwanted glaze with a clean cloth immediately. Remove most of the glaze from the center of the panel and from highlighted parts of the framing, but leave some in depressions. Work with the cloth to get the desired effect. If you overdo the wiping, apply more glaze and wipe again.

Wiping with the cloth should give the general effect wanted, but there will be marks from the cloth and a general roughness of definition of the glaze color edges. To even out these marks, use a large, dry brush. Stroke it over the work, always working from a lighter to a darker area. On a panel, brush from the center to the sides. On framing, however, you will need to regulate the direction of movement to suit the disposition of the light and dark parts. Clean the brush by wiping occasionally with cloth. You can vary the brushing action on some parts by working the brush up and down on the surface while you hold it vertically.

Look at the work from all directions and see that the glaze color changes gradually and that emphasis is given where it is wanted. Be careful not to smudge the work by handling. There will probably be signs of the glaze in depressions of the main color, even in parts that have been wiped the most. This is part of the antiquing and should be left. It all builds up the appearance of age in the furniture. Leave the glaze to dry completely, at least overnight, then apply a clear finish over it. The clear finish may be white shellac or clear lacquer. After it dries, rub it down lightly with fine abrasive or steel wool. Follow with wax polish.

You can use a similar antiquing treatment over a clear finish. The wood can be bare or stained. First, lacquer or French-polish the surface, over filler if necessary. Use only one or two coats before antiquing. The glaze can be one of those suggested for a painted finish. Apply the glaze as described, just wiping and brushing to get the effect desired. In carved or other shaped parts, remove glaze from the higher parts and leave it in the recesses, but do not leave an excess that will accumulate on the surface when dry.

Finish the antiqued surface after drying with coats of shellac or clear lacquer. Rub it down with an abrasive and polish with wax polish.

If the finish is to be antiqued gold or silver, follow the directions that come with the gold or silver mixture. It is possible to buy the powders to mix with a special bronzing liquid to make a pint. Normally, you will seal the wood, possibly with shellac, and apply one or two coats of undercoat paint appropriate to the finish. Keep the gold or silver mixture stirred and have it thick enough to cover in one operation. Let it dry, then coat it with shellac. Use a burnt umber glaze over gold or a lampblack glaze over silver, applying and shading as already described.

Gold and silver bronzes are available in aerosol containers. It is also possible to get lacquer shading stains, which can be used for antiquing, but spraying must be done exactly where wanted since the sprayed lacquer cannot be wiped or brushed.

USING PLASTER

There was a demand, particularly in Victorian days, for wood decorated with plaster, which was then given a gold or silver finish. Although paints were used, some of the coating was actually gold leaf. Picture frames were the most common things treated in this way, but the technique was also used on other woodwork.

Plaster of paris does not have much resistance to damage, so old furniture treated in this way is likely to have damaged parts. If you cannot obtain plaster of paris at a hardware store, a more refined, expensive type is available at drugstores. Experiment before doing an actual repair. Setting is very quick, so make all your preparations before you add water to the plaster powder. Stir in water to a thick, creamy consistency. Mix only a little at a time. Once it sets, whether on the wood or in the pit, nothing can be done to make it liquid again.

Mixing is best done in a throwaway container—old cans, plastic jars, etc. Mix with a piece of wood that can then be used to lift blobs of liquid plaster onto the repair.

For most repairs, you will need to place plaster in position and mold it into shape with a stick, knife blade, or other tool. It might help, particularly along a straight edge, to use a piece of plywood or card to keep the plaster within bounds (FIG. 21-5). To prevent the plaster from sticking to the plywood, coat it with wax or grease.

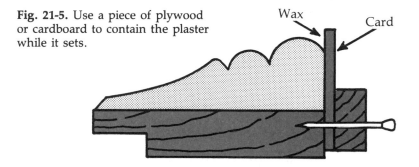

Fig. 21-5. Use a piece of plywood or cardboard to contain the plaster while it sets.

Wax

Card

Much of this plasterwork is in the form of molding, often with beads. When made originally, beads would have been cast in a mold, giving uniform patterns. Things like free-flowing curves, stylized leaves, and even straight flutes are not too difficult to shape with hand tools. It is difficult, however, to get a true spherical shape for the series of knobs forming beads. It might be easier to find round shot or other little spheres and press them into the plaster (FIG. 21-6).

You can expect to have up to 5 minutes working time, so you need to work quickly and carefully. Leave the plaster a little too thick anywhere that you do not think you can get exact. You can shape the dried plaster by sanding. With abrasive paper wrapped around wood and used like a file, you can work the surface to match adjoining areas.

Dry plaster is extremely absorbent. If you will brush or spray on a gold or silver mixture, first seal the surface with several coats of shellac. Finishing then is as already described. Antiquing may follow.

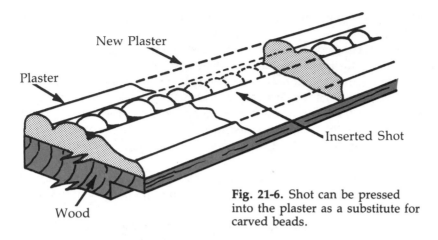

Fig. 21-6. Shot can be pressed into the plaster as a substitute for carved beads.

USING GOLD LEAF

You can use gold leaf over plaster or wood to make a matching repair. Successful application can be difficult, however, and the use of a liquid mixture is much simpler. Nevertheless, there is nothing to equal gold leaf in appearance, and the real thing might be the only way of making a proper repair.

Gold leaf is supplied in the form of 20 small pages of a book. The gold has been rolled or hammered extremely thin—0.001 inch is the thickness you will be handling. There are fine, sharp gilder's knives, but you can do the same work with a razor blade, preferably in a handle. The gold is not picked up by the fingers, but is lifted by a *gilder's tip*, which is a thin flat brush with long hairs. Gold leaf is applied with an adhesive.

If the gold leaf is to go over parts adjoining the repair, check that the surfaces are clean. You can use detergent, but be sure to remove it with clean water. If the plaster or wood absorbs water, allow it to dry completely before proceeding. Apply several coats of shellac to any bare plaster. Lightly sand it smooth. Clean off dust. Small lumps on the surface might show through. Coat surfaces that are to take gold leaf with the adhesive and allow them to get tacky. The waiting time is about 2 hours.

Cut the gold leaf to approximate shapes, but edges should overlap. Pick up a piece with the gilder's tip and put it in place over the adhesive. Coax it down with the tip of the brush. Do this with pieces of leaf all over the surface. Use small pieces of leaf to fill any gaps. Make sure all leaf is in close contact with the adhesive. Although the thin gold will adapt to shapes, smaller pieces are easier to fix over intricate designs. Use the gilder's tip to position the leaves, not your hand or any other tool.

To give the finished surface a more even appearance and a semblance of age, place a little gold bronze powder on a cloth, and lightly rub it over the surface. Allow a day for everything to dry hard before any further treatment. The repair will probably benefit from a coat of shellac to protect it.

BAMBOO FURNITURE

The normal wood of a tree gains a layer on the outside each year; bamboo starts as an outside tube and grows inside. This means that the strong wood is on the outside. In most bamboo used for furniture, this hard outside skin is also smooth and glossy when new. In any bamboo repair, it is inadvisable to break through this skin since its destruction might mean weakening, possibly out of proportion to the actual amount removed.

You can strip and clean bamboo furniture in the same way as other wood furniture. If there are any hollow ends exposed, avoid letting stripper enter and become trapped: it might harm the core. Some sanding might be needed, but avoid sanding excessively. In any case, bamboo has a certain character and the aim of restoring is to renew or emphasize this character.

RESTORING METALS

Metal furniture is often made of iron or steel. Very old blacksmith-made furniture will almost certainly have been made of wrought iron, which has a good resistance to rust. Newer furniture is made of mild steel, which is much more prone to rust. Initial rusting tends to make a barrier to further attack, but neglected steel furniture might be riddled with rust and so eaten away that not enough sound steel is left to justify restoring. Painting over rust is only disguising the trouble temporarily. Rust will continue under the paint and soon show through as brown marks.

You can strip painted iron or steel furniture with wood strippers. Since there is no grain, the paint might come away easier. You can also use a wire brush, either a hand type or a rotating one driven by a power drill. In both cases, you need one with spring steel "bristles."

It is impossible to remove every bit of rust. Instead, work on the surface until it is generally bright; there might be some pitting still containing rust. Do not leave the surface at this stage. A bright, smooth steel surface will acquire a new film of rust overnight, even in an apparently dry atmosphere.

Paint on a rust-inhibiting fluid, which prevents rust from spreading and discourages further rusting. Follow the manufacturer's instructions, particularly about the time to be left before painting over.

Painting iron or steel furniture is simple: there are undercoats to provide a base and a top coat. Since the metal is not absorbent, be careful not to leave excess paint anywhere. Excess will be likely to run and leave unsightly blobs.

Normally there is no need to start with any special paint for a first coat on wood furniture. For iron or steel furniture that is to remain outdoors, however, some paint manufacturers offer special primers that etch their way into the surface to get a grip on the metal and provide a longer lasting paint base.

Old metal fittings usually did not have an applied finish originally; any quality of appearance was a result of the smoothing of the metal itself. Iron hinges and fastenings on an antique chest might have had a coat of paint but nonferrous metal fittings, usually loosely described as *brass*, probably had polished surfaces. Brass is a copper/zinc alloy. Bronzes could be copper/tin, or they could be the same as brass with the addition of a small quantity of some other metal. Most old brasses have a more golden color than new brass, indicating a higher proportion of copper in the alloy. So it is not always satisfactory to replace an old fitting with the only equivalent obtainable today.

The first step in dealing with a dirty old fitting after you have removed it from the furniture is to look at its back, which will be cleaner and provide a clue to the alloy. You can scrape off paint or polish that has gone over the edges, but be careful to avoid cutting into the metal. Some old alloys are quite soft. Scrub with water and detergent to remove dirt. If there is wax from wood polish, dissolve it with turpentine or thinners.

When you have removed all of the buildup on the surface, the surface will still be dull. This dullness will be corrosion—the equivalent of rust on iron. It is not usually more than just an even coating on the surface, however. It is possible to clean off the corrosion with acid, but although the result is rapid, this can be dangerous because the metal must be soaked in a fairly strong solution of acid. Another way is to use an ammonia solution. Avoid breathing the fumes while inserting or removing the article from the solution. Leave until you can see that the metal has been cleaned—about 20 minutes. Then wash off the ammonia in running water and dry the metal.

If a polish is to be built up and the surface is not evenly clean from the ammonia treatment, use fine steel wool followed by a damp cloth or a scrubbing brush with pumice powder or domestic cleaning powder. This step should reduce the surface to an even appearance.

Polish on bare metal is the result of working on the surface with successively finer abrasives, with each completely removing traces of work of the previous stage. Pumice powder is the first stage. There must be no traces of pumice left and the surface must be dry. Follow with a cloth or brush and a liquid polish of the type intended for brass. This procedure might be sufficient to give a satisfactory finish, but for the highest polish on any metal, follow with a polish intended for silver.

Power polishing is much quicker than hand polishing, but there is a risk of rounding edges and taking off decorative ridges and beads. This is one way of simulating the wear of age, but machine wear might not follow the same lines as natural wear and therefore not be regarded as authentic. Power polishing is best done with a *mop*, consisting of a large number of cloth disks on a spindle rotating at a high speed. To create enough pressure, a 6-inch diameter mop needs to turn at about 3000 rpm. Use a polishing compound with a coarse cut for first polishing, but soon change to finer compounds. Have the mop turning toward you and hold the metal sloping downward. Pause frequently to allow the mop to cool. Do not dip it in water.

Of course, polished metal will become dull again after exposure to the air. At one time, the only solution possible was repolishing at intervals. The alternative today is to spray with clear lacquer. This can be the same lacquer used for a clear finish on wood, but there are also special transparent lacquers intended for use on metal. These lacquers dry to an almost invisible hard film to prevent the atmosphere from causing dulling of the surface.

Index